Great Leaders, Thinkers, and Coaches on Marshall Goldsmith and *The Earned Life*

In my fifty-year career as an executive educator and coach, I have been blessed to work with many of the greatest leaders in America. In theory, I am supposed to teach them. In practice, I have learned far more from them than they have learned from me. The leaders, thinkers, and coaches below have been gracious enough to endorse my work and The Earned Life. *To help readers understand their profound accomplishments, I have added my own comments in italics below each person's quotation. By sharing what I have learned, I hope this book can help you in the way that these great leaders, thinkers, and coaches have helped me.*

—MARSHALL GOLDSMITH

* * *

"My life changed for the better when I started working with Marshall Goldsmith. Since then, all of my significant decisions have been influenced by his wisdom, compassion, and commitment. In his 100 Coaches community, we all encourage one another to move toward fulfillment and away from regret. As you read this wonderful book, *The Earned Life,* try to hear Marshall's voice. Know you can face the challenges ahead and start anew. I hear this soundtrack every day as I go out, with humility and passion, to earn my life once again."

—DR. JIM YONG KIM, served as president of the World Bank

As a founder of Partners in Health, and then president of the World Bank, Jim led humanitarian efforts that had a dramatic impact in developing countries and saved tens of millions of lives.

* * *

"The essence of Marshall Goldsmith's coaching is in his dedication to his purpose, which is to help each and every one of his clients, including me, find happiness and fulfillment—and to be even better for themselves and the people they lead. And now, he's broadening the scope beyond his clients to everyone who reads this book. What a gift from him to us—to help us become the people that we want to be and to live a fulfilled life with no regrets. Thank you, Marshall—*The Earned Life* rocks!"   —ALAN MULALLY, served as CEO, Ford

As the CEO of Boeing Commercial Airlines after the 9/11 terrorist attacks, and then the CEO of Ford after the financial crisis, Alan led two of America's most successful and inspiring corporate success stories in the face of incredible challenges.

*   *   *

"Through his wonderful coaching and friendship, Marshall Goldsmith has no doubt helped me to become both a better leader and a happier person. Perhaps the most profound impact he has had on me is helping me learn to embrace feedback—to learn how I am seen, then practice feedforward—to make positive change. In *The Earned Life*, the world's most admired coach shares some of his most valuable and impactful insights into creating a happy and fulfilling life."

—HUBERT JOLY, served as CEO, Best Buy

When Hubert joined Best Buy, it was predicted to go bankrupt. After his eight-year tenure as CEO, the company achieved phenomenal growth and profitability. This amazing story is captured in his bestselling book, The Heart of Business.

*   *   *

"Our lives are filled with many wonderful things and, for me, Marshall Goldsmith is one of them. From the first day we met and began our work together when I was CEO of the Girl Scouts until today, Marshall has been such a special part of my life and work. And now, with *The Earned Life*, Marshall shares with all of us, something that is so important, which is just how we can live a fulfilled life. You must read this masterpiece!"

—FRANCES HESSELBEIN, served as CEO, Girl Scouts of the USA

As CEO of the Girl Scouts, Frances's impact was so spectacular that she was awarded the Presidential Medal of Freedom for her leadership. The legendary Peter Drucker declared her to be "The greatest executive I have ever met."

*   *   *

"Marshall Goldsmith has the unique ability to speak with me for five minutes and provide thought-provoking insights on how to lead and grow, while keeping me centered on what is important. It is quite amazing. During the COVID-19 pandemic, as Pfizer continues to play a critical role in helping protect and save lives, I have leaned on Marshall even more; not only to speak about work-related issues, but just to chat about life. He is a wonderful coach, educator, and author."

—ALBERT BOURLA, CEO, Pfizer

As CEO of Pfizer, Albert has tirelessly led the company in the face of one of the greatest challenges to humanity in our lifetime, the COVID pandemic. Pfizer's amazing success is unprecedented in the history of drug development.

* * *

"Marshall Goldsmith is a sage for the modern world. He brings his honesty, compassion, and wisdom to every book, every speech, every meeting, and every interaction that I have had with him."

—ASHEESH ADVANI, CEO, Junior Achievement Worldwide

Junior Achievement has been nominated for the 2022 Nobel Peace Prize for their work in economically empowering youth around the world.

* * *

"Marshall Goldsmith's unique approach to coaching has not only challenged me, it has also inspired me to be a better leader and a better person. With his new book, *The Earned Life,* Marshall will walk you through the process of developing a purpose-driven life. The philosophical and practical approaches in this book will challenge you in the same way that Marshall has challenged me."

—JAMES DOWNING, president and CEO,
St. Jude Children's Research Hospital

A pediatric oncologist, Downing in 2014 was named the leader of St. Jude's, a world leader in battling pediatric cancer.

* * *

"*The Earned Life* is a great addition to Marshall's body of work. The advice in this book can help you keep on achieving and, at the same time, do a better job of finding peace and happiness in the process."

—AMY EDMONSON, Novartis Professor of Leadership
and Management, Harvard Business School

In 2021 Amy was named the Thinkers50 #1 Most Influential Management Thinker in the World.

*   *   *

"Marshall Goldsmith pierces right to the center of things. For anyone who wishes to align their efforts with a life of meaning, Marshall is a fabulous companion, guide, and cheerleader. For those who don't know him personally, how lucky you are that you can now grow from reading this book!" —JOHN DICKERSON, CBS News chief political analyst

John contributes his reporting across CBS's news programming, including Sunday Morning *and the* CBS Evening News. *He is the author of the bestseller* The Hardest Job in the World.

*   *   *

"Every day I focus on being grateful for every moment. I am so goal-oriented that I can forget that happiness and achievement do not have to be mutually exclusive. By being present, I can remind myself to be more selfless in the decisions I make. Marshall Goldsmith has been a great coach in helping me grow up and do just this!"

—DAVID CHANG, chef and author

The founder of groundbreaking restaurant Momofuku, Dave is a James Beard Award winner, media personality, and author of the bestselling memoir Eat a Peach.

*   *   *

"Working with Marshall Goldsmith has been a blessing. He continues to help me become a better person, a better wife, a better mom, and a better leader. My journey with him has been nothing short of a joy, even in the face of having to make fundamental changes. *The Earned Life* perfectly captures his spirit and the impact he has had on so many of us." —AICHA EVANS, CEO, Zoox

Formerly senior vice president and chief strategy officer at Intel Corporation, Aicha was named to Fortune's 2021 Most Powerful Women in Business "Ones to Watch" list.

*   *   *

"I just finished reading *The Earned Life*. Thank you for this beautiful invitation to a deeper conversation with myself!"

—NANKHONDE VAN DEN BROEK,
executive coach, activist, and entrepreneur

Nankhonde was named the 2021 Thinkers50 Most Influential Leadership Coach in the World.

*   *   *

"In *The Earned Life*, Marshall Goldsmith has brilliantly captured principles we learned in more than four hundred hours of intimate weekend conversations with sixty of the most extraordinary people in the world."   —MARK C. THOMPSON, leadership coach

Mark is the bestselling author of Admired *and* Success Built to Last. *A top-rated CEO coach, he is a Thinkers50 Top Ten Executive Coach.*

*   *   *

"I've been incredibly fortunate to have met Marshall Goldsmith, to have him as part of my life, and to have been able to learn from him— along with learning from the many other exceptional people in his 100 Coaches community. He has played a very important role in my transition from being a professional athlete to beginning the next chapter in my life."   —PAU GASOL, former NBA All-Star

Pau is a two-time NBA champion, five-time Olympian (with three medals), and president of the Gasol Foundation.

*   *   *

"Who else but Marshall Goldsmith could get leaders from around the world to look forward to Zoom calls on the weekends? He convenes an impressive collection of people from every sector of our economy to share, learn, and most importantly 'pay it forward.' In his 100 Coaches community, I find the common thread of our discussions to be 'leading with humanity.' I am certain that you will learn from *The Earned Life* and be encouraged to join all of us in paying it forward with the insights you gain!"

—MICHELLE SEITZ, chairman and CEO, Russell Investments

Since being named CEO in 2017, Michelle has led one of the world's largest and most successful investment firms.

*   *   *

"Marshall Goldsmith is a life-changer. For the past decade, he's remained a pivotal advisor through every step of my career. I feel privileged to be a part of his 100 Coaches community. Marshall makes the complex simple, inspires you to get better every day, and challenges you to create positive change that endures. In, *The Earned Life,* his most important book yet, he reminds us that bold ambition can be a tyranny, if we anchor our identities to constant goal achievement. We have to relish the journey and our own happiness—it is the most important choice we need to make."

—MARGO GEORGIADIS, served as president and CEO, Ancestry

Before leading the incredible transformation of Ancestry, Margo was the CEO of Mattel and has been recognized as one of the 50 Most Powerful Women in Business.

*   *   *

"Marshall Goldsmith is a brilliant mentor who truly helps you be happier and wiser. He has helped so many—including me. He is a force multiplier for good. I can't wait for readers to exponentially make a positive difference in the world because of what they will learn in *The Earned Life.*"   —SANYIN SIANG, CEO coach, advisor, and author

The founding executive director of Duke University's Coach K Leadership & Ethics Center at its Fuqua School of Business, Sanyin is a Thinkers50 #1 Coach and author of The Launch Book.

*   *   *

"I've had the incredible honor of being a member of Marshall Goldsmith's distinguished community of leaders. His ability to illuminate the humanity in each of us is truly extraordinary. He gets to the core of any matter, personal or professional, and fosters an affirming and productive environment. The vulnerability of members in our community leaves us motivated and inspired."

—SARAH HIRSHLAND, CEO of the USA Olympic
and Paralympic Committee

The former senior vice president for strategic business development at Wasserman, Sarah led Team USA to a successful run at the Tokyo Olympics after assuming leadership at USOPC in 2018.

*   *   *

"*The Earned Life* is Marshall Goldsmith at his best. Insightful, empathic, and practical, all at the same time. This book can help you have a more complete and fulfilling life."

—JEFF PFEFFER, Thomas D. Dee II Professor of Organizational
Behavior at the Graduate School of Business, Stanford University

A professor at Stanford since 1970, Jeff has published more than fifteen books, including Dying for a Paycheck *and* The Knowing-Doing Gap.

*   *   *

"Marshall Goldsmith never pulls his punches or curbs his wonderful wit. He sees our flaws and leads us to do better, with cajoling or stories, and then with a friendly two-by-four of insight, especially handy for those of us who need less subtlety. *The Earned Life* and Marshall's other writing and speaking have made him truly the world's coach."

—TONY MARX, president and CEO, New York Public Library

The former president of Amherst College, Tony became the president of the New York Public Library in 2011, spearheading a number of innovative initiatives.

*   *   *

"More than anyone I know, Marshall Goldsmith makes the impossible possible. Without him, I wouldn't be where I am today. He has helped make my life both more enriching and more fun. I hope that *The Earned Life* will help you in the same way Marshall has helped me!"

—MARTIN LINDSTROM, author and consumer branding expert

Martin is the founder of Lindstrom Company, the bestselling author of Buyology *and* Small Data, *and was named one of the TIME100 Most Influential People. He is the world's no. 1 authority on branding.*

*   *   *

"Over the years, Marshall Goldsmith has become one of the greatest leadership thinkers in the world and yet he has continued to be one of the finest, most caring human beings I know. He lives to the fullest. *The Earned Life* will help you do the same."

—KEN BLANCHARD, author, speaker, and business consultant

An iconic, beloved, and respected management educator, Ken is one of the most popular nonfiction authors in history, with over twenty-three million books sold.

*　　*　　*

"Marshall Goldsmith has transformed the lives of thousands of people for the better, mine included! He is a humanist—a wonderfully funny person who is very serious about helping people. A humble monk, he brings opposing qualities together to create deep and timeless value."

—AYSE BIRSEL, designer and author

Named by Fast Company as one of the 100 Most Creative People in Business, Ayse is a Thinkers50 Top Ten Coach and author of Design the Life You Love.

*　　*　　*

"As a coach and advisor, Marshall Goldsmith has a knack for suggesting just the right tweak at the right time. *The Earned Life* is a wonderful book." —RITA MCGRATH, professor, Columbia Business School

One of the world's top experts on innovation, Rita was named Thinkers50 #1 Strategic Thinker and is the author of Seeing Around Corners.

*　　*　　*

"Marshall Goldsmith's brilliance and generosity of spirt delight all who meet him. His teaching and coaching, as shared in *The Earned Life*, can also make you be a better person. Never miss the chance to have a 'Marshall Goldsmith experience'!"

—CHESTER ELTON and ADRIAN GOSTICK, authors

Chester and Adrian are the New York Times *bestselling authors of* All In *and* Leading with Gratitude.

*　　*　　*

"In *The Earned Life*, Marshall Goldsmith distills his vast coaching experience into an insightful and inspiring guide to help you avoid regret and lead a life of fulfillment."

—SAFI BAHCALL, physicist, entrepreneur, and author

Safi worked with President Obama's Council on Science and Technology and is the author of the #1 Wall Street Journal *bestseller* Loonshots.

*   *   *

"In *The Earned Life*, Marshall Goldsmith helps us 'let it go.' With unfailing compassion and wisdom, he shows us how to move from regret to fulfillment—no matter what our age or stage in life."

—SALLY HELGESEN, coach and author

Sally was named Forbes World #1 Coach for Women Leaders and is the author of the bestseller How Women Rise.

*   *   *

"Marshall Goldsmith has given me the gift of helping me change possibility into reality. Read this book. I hope that it can do the same for you."   —WHITNEY JOHNSON, CEO, Disruption Advisors

Whitney was named a Thinkers50 Top Ten Management Thinker and is the author of Smart Growth.

*   *   *

"*The Earned Life* is the friendly hand that can help you live the life you truly want—or bat you on the side of your head when you turn your back on yourself."   —CAROL KAUFFMAN, founder,
Institute of Coaching, Harvard Medical School

Carol is a Thinkers50 Top Ten Executive Coach.

*   *   *

"Marshall Goldsmith has done it again. *The Earned Life* contains insights and tools that make you feel like Marshall is personally coaching you."   —DAVID ULRICH, Rensis Likert Professor,
Ross School of Business, University of Michigan

David is the world's #1 HR Thinker, noted author, and member of the Thinkers50 Hall of Fame.

THE EARNED LIFE

The

EARNED
LIFE

LOSE REGRET, CHOOSE FULFILLMENT

MARSHALL
GOLDSMITH

and **Mark Reiter**

CURRENCY

Published in the United States by Currency, an imprint of Random House, a division of Penguin Random House LLC, New York.

CURRENCY and its colophon are trademarks of Penguin Random House LLC.

LIBRARY OF CONGRESS CATALOGING-IN-PUBLICATION DATA
Names: Goldsmith, Marshall, author. | Reiter, Mark, author.
Title: The earned life / Marshall Goldsmith and Mark Reiter.
Description: First edition. | New York : Currency, [2022] |
Includes index.
Identifiers: LCCN 2022000141 (print) | LCCN 2022000142 (ebook) |
ISBN 9780593237274 (hardcover) | ISBN 9780593443361 |
ISBN 9780593237281 (ebook) |
ISBN 9780593237281 (international edition)
Subjects: LCSH: Self-actualization (Psychology) |
Motivation (Psychology) | Regret.
Classification: LCC BF637.S4 G55 2022 (print) | LCC BF637.S4 (ebook)
| DDC 158.1—dc23/eng/20220114
LC record available at https://lccn.loc.gov/2022000141
LC ebook record available at https://lccn.loc.gov/2022000142

Printed in the United States of America on acid-free paper

crownpublishing.com

2nd Printing

First Edition

Illustrations by Nigel Holmes
Title page illustration by thedafkish/Getty Images

To Dr. R. Roosevelt Thomas, Jr. (1944–2013),
for his insights and support,

and

Annik LaFarge, for bringing us together

Presume not that I am the thing that I was.

—*Henry V*, William Shakespeare

CONTENTS

INTRODUCTION

———

SOME YEARS AGO, during the George W. Bush administration, I was introduced to a man named Richard at a leadership conference. Richard was a business manager for artists, writers, and musicians. Several mutual acquaintances had told me Richard and I had much in common. He lived in New York City, where I had just bought an apartment, and we agreed to get together for dinner the next time I was in town. At the last minute, he bailed out for no apparent reason. Oh well.

A few years later—during the Obama administration—we finally got together for dinner and, as friends had predicted, immediately hit it off. Lots of spirited discussion and laughs. At some point Richard expressed contrition about canceling on me way back when, imagining all the good times and jovial meals we'd missed out on during, as he put it, those "wasted years" before we met. He was joking about the "wasted years," of course, but he couldn't conceal a shade of melancholy, as if he had bungled a life decision that required an apology.

He'd periodically repeat that note of contrition the two or three times a year we'd get together in New York. Each time, I'd say, "Let it go. I accept your apology." Then, during one of our dinners, he told me a story.

He had just graduated from high school in a Maryland suburb.

An indifferent student and not yet interested in college, he enlisted in the U.S. Army. After three years of service, at a military base in Germany rather than in combat deployment to Vietnam, he returned to Maryland, determined to get a college degree. He was twenty-one and finally clear-eyed about his future. He spent the summer before his freshman year driving a cab around the Washington, D.C., area. One day his fare from the airport to Bethesda was a young woman, a student at Brown returning from a year of study abroad in Germany.

"We had an hour in traffic to compare notes about Germany," Richard explained. "It was one of the most charming hours of my life up to that point. There was definitely chemistry in that cab. When we pulled up to her parents' very large house I carried her bags to the porch, stalling so I could figure out my next move. I wanted to see her again, but a driver asking a passenger out on a date was frowned upon, so I did the next best thing. I wrote my name on a taxi company card and smoothly said, 'If you need a ride to the airport, call the dispatcher and ask for me.'

"She said, 'I'd like that,' making it sound like we were already agreeing on a date. I floated back to the cab, high on the possibilities. She knew how to reach me and I knew where she lived; we were connected in some small way."

As Richard spoke, I was sure I knew where his story was going. It was the raw material for nearly every romantic comedy I'd ever seen. Girl and boy meet, one of them loses a name or number or address, the other waits in vain to hear from them again, by happenstance they run into each other years later and reconnect. Or some variation thereof.

"She called a few days later and we set up a date the next weekend," Richard continued. "I drove to her house and stopped three blocks away to collect myself. This evening was important to me. I could see spending my life with her, despite the fact that she came from a much more well-to-do background than mine. And then I did something inexplicable. I froze. Maybe it was the big house or the swanky neighborhood or the fact that I drove a cab, but I couldn't work up the courage to walk up to her door. I never saw her again—and my cowardice has haunted me for forty years. It has to be a big reason why I've spent my entire adult life alone."

Richard's voice choked up with this abrupt and baffling ending to his story. His face was so anguished, I had to look away. I had expected either a heartwarming reminiscence about a successful first date and many more to follow, or a bittersweet admission that after a few dates he and the young woman realized they weren't the soulmates they had hoped they were. Instead, I had heard a narrative of colossal regret, that empty and most desolate of human emotions. It was a conversation stopper that landed between us with a tragic thud. I had nothing healing or redemptive to add. Regret is a feeling I wouldn't wish on any human being.

ANY DECENT ADVICE book aims to help readers overcome a perennial challenge. Losing weight, getting rich, and finding love are three universal challenges that come to mind. The focus in my recent books has been on our behavior at the nexus where our professional aspirations intersect with our personal well-being. In *What Got You Here Won't Get You There*, I tackled how to eradicate self-defeating behavior in the workplace; in *Mojo*, how to deal with career setbacks that stop our momentum; and in *Triggers*, how to recognize the everyday situations that trigger our least appealing responses and choices.

The challenge we're tackling here is regret.

My premise is that our lives toggle back and forth between two emotional polarities. At one pole is the emotion we know as "fulfillment." We judge our internal sense of fulfillment against six factors that I call the Fulfillers:

- Purpose
- Meaning
- Achievement
- Relationships
- Engagement
- Happiness

These are the guideposts that dictate all our striving in life.* We invest enormous resources of time and energy to find purpose and meaning in our lives, to be recognized for our achievement, to maintain our relationships, to be engaged in whatever we do, and to be happy. Our vigilance and striving here are unceasing, because our connection to these six factors is fragile, fickle, and fleeting.

Happiness, for example, is the universal temperature reading of our emotional well-being, which is why we frequently ask ourselves whether we're happy, or endure the question from others. Yet happiness can be our least permanent emotional state, as brief

---

* I have intentionally excluded health and wealth from this list of Fulfillers—surely two additional major areas of all our striving—under the assumption that if you're reading this book, these two objectives have already occupied much of your adult life, to the point where you may have each under control. You look in the mirror or at your bank statement and tell yourself, "I'm good." Mostly, though, I'm convinced that if you're in need of diet, fitness, and get-rich advice, you'll find better answers elsewhere.

as a dream. Our nose itches, we scratch it, we're relieved and happy, then we notice an annoying fly buzzing around the room and a chilly breeze gusting through the window, and somewhere a leaky faucet is dripping. This goes on from moment to moment all day long. Our happiness vanishes instantly and constantly. Meaning, purpose, engagement, relationships, and achievement are equally vulnerable. We reach for them and grasp them, but with alarming rapidity they slip through our fingers.

We think that if we can create an equivalence between (a) the choices, risks, and effort we made in pursuing the six Fulfillers *and* (b) the reward we received for doing so, we will achieve a lasting sense of fulfillment—as if we've discovered that our world is fair and just. We remind ourselves, *I wanted it, I worked for it, and my reward was equal to my effort. In other words, I earned it.* It is a simple dynamic that describes much of our striving in life. But as we shall see, it offers us an incomplete picture of an earned life.

REGRET IS THE polar opposite of fulfillment.

Regret, in the words of Kathryn Schulz in her wonderful 2011 TED talk on the subject, is "the emotion we experience when we think that our present situation could be better or happier if we had done something different in the past." Regret is a devilish cocktail of *agency* (our regrets are ours to create, they're not foisted upon us by others) and *imagination* (we have to visualize making a different choice in our past that delivers a more appealing outcome now). Regret is totally within our control, at least in terms of how often we invite it into our lives and how long we let it stick around. Do we choose to be tortured or bewildered by it forever (as in the case of my friend Richard), or can we move on, knowing that regret is not finished with us, that we will surely live to regret again someday?

Our regrets are not one-size-fits-all. Like men's shirts, they come in S, M, L, XL, XXL, and even bigger. To be clear, in this book I'm not going to be concerning myself with microregrets, incidental missteps such as the slip of the tongue that offends a colleague. These are regrettable faux pas usually resolved with a sincere apology. Nor am I thinking about our medium-sized regrets such as the tattoo that inspired Kathryn Schulz's TED talk, tormenting her the moment she left the tattoo parlor, obsessively wondering, "What was I thinking?" Eventually she got over it, even gleaned a lesson about how "exposed" and "totally uninsured" she was from her regrettable choices—and promised herself to do better in the future.

What we're addressing here is supersized existential regret, the kind that reroutes destinies and persecutes our memory for decades. Existential regret is deciding not to have children, then changing our mind too late. It's allowing our soulmate to become "the one who got away." It's turning down the perfect job because we doubt ourselves far more than do the folks who want to hire us. It's not taking our studies seriously in school. It's looking back in retirement and wishing we'd allowed ourselves more leisure time to develop interests outside work.

It can be hard but it's not impossible to avoid existential regret—as long we're open to focusing on our fulfillment. Being open to opportunities that come our way can help us avoid regret, even when we believe we're already happy and fulfilled where we are. The simplest tool I know to finding fulfillment is being open to fulfillment.

Readers of my previous books know that I am incapable of concealing my admiration for my friend Alan Mulally. I consider Alan a role model for creating a life blessed with fulfillment and zero regret.

In 2006, when Alan was CEO of Boeing Commercial Airplanes and was offered the CEO job at Ford Motor Company, he sought my advice about the pros and cons of leaving Boeing, the only company he'd ever worked for. As his former coach, I felt I was in a uniquely objective position to advise him. I knew that he was an exceptional leader and believed he could succeed in any executive role. I also had known for some time that he would be given multiple opportunities to lead at other companies, although very few of them would be sufficiently appealing or challenging to lure him away from Boeing. Any offer would have to be an extraordinary opportunity to serve. Helping revive Ford was such an opportunity, and I reminded Alan of previous career advice I'd given to him: *Be open.*

Alan initially declined the Ford offer. But he kept an open mind and continued to gather information about what would be required to reinvigorate the auto giant, reconsidering the job from all sides (it's one of his talents). A few days later, he accepted the offer to serve at Ford. In doing so, he continued to focus on being open to achieving even greater fulfillment, not avoiding regret.*

Regret, however, is our secondary theme here. I flirted with titling this book "The Regret Cure" but concluded that that would be misleading. Regret is the stranger knocking on the door, appearing when we make poor choices and everything has gone awry. It is the thing to avoid, keeping in mind that we cannot banish it

---

*Ford's stock price increased 1,837 percent during Alan's seven-year tenure as CEO and, more important, he had a 97 percent CEO approval rating from employees at a unionized company.

entirely (nor should we, considering how instructive our regrets can be: "Note to self: Don't do *that* again!"). Our official policy on regret in these pages is to accept its inevitability but reduce its frequency. Regret is the depressing counterweight to finding fulfillment in a complex world. Our primary theme is achieving a life of fulfillment—what I call an *earned life*.

ONE OF OUR guiding concepts here is that our lives reside on a continuum that roams between Regret and Fulfillment, as illustrated below.

Regret   Fulfillment

Given the choice, each of us I'm sure would prefer spending more time approaching the right extreme here than the left. In researching this book, I asked a wide variety of people in my professional circle to locate themselves on this continuum. It's hardly a rigorous scientific study, but I was curious about what propelled people to place themselves closer to fulfillment than regret, and if so, how close. My respondents were all successful by the obvious metrics we rely on. They were healthy. They had accumulated a credible list of professional achievements, as well as the status, money, and respect that tend to accompany achievement. I figured most of them would come very close to the extreme right of the line; all the signs said they should be experiencing near-total fulfillment.

Silly me. The truth is, none of us knows the scale of another man or woman's aspirations and therefore none of us knows the depth of his or her disappointments and regrets. We can neither presume nor predict other people's relationship to fulfillment or regret, even those we think we know well. Here is the response of a European CEO named Gunther who's at the top of his field and yet overwhelmed by regret for neglecting his family in favor of his career:

Regret   Fulfillment

Pressed to measure his sense of fulfillment, Gunther saw that all the conventional metrics of success at which he excelled could not counteract his sense of failure as a parent and husband. The failure overwhelmed his success, as if he'd wasted his life earning the wrong rewards.

It was the same story with my coaching client Aarin. I regarded her as a roaring overachiever—and therefore an amply satisfied woman with few regrets. Aarin had emigrated from Nigeria to the United States at age eleven, earned an advanced degree in civil engineering, and developed a specific expertise that made her an in-demand consultant in the construction of skyscrapers, bridges, tunnels, and other big structures. She was in her early fifties, happily married, with two college-age children. As an African immigrant, she was a rarity in her line of work, possibly the only one, which meant that she had basically invented a career for herself. I admired that. I'd been coaching her for six years under the impression that I knew both her dreams and resentments. So her relatively downbeat response surprised me.

Regret   Fulfillment

How could she, of all people, be more regretful than ful-filled? She had a "baseline satisfaction" with her life, she said. "I have no reason to complain." And yet she was swamped by regret. Her regrets centered not on how far she'd come but rather on how little she'd done compared with what she believed she could be doing. No matter what she did, she couldn't shake the thought that she was falling short of her potential. She regretted that when she took on a project that paid well enough to cover overhead and salaries, she tended to coast and ease up on chasing new business. Why, she wondered, didn't she hire people to handle multiple projects at the same time and give herself more time for rainmaking? "Everyone thinks I'm this hard-charger," she said. "But I'm actually a sheep in Type A clothing. Most days I feel like an impostor, unworthy of the fees I'm charging and the praise I receive, always dreading the moment when I'll be found out."

Clearly, we had more coaching to do.

I was surprised when any of the responses in my admittedly arbitrary and unscientific survey resembled Gunther's and Aarin's answers. People who could be seen as paragons of fulfillment turned out to be tormented by persistent regret.

I expected all of them to be like Leonard, a Wall Street trader who'd been forced into retirement at age forty-six when his type of highly leveraged trading became a casualty of the Dodd-Frank financial reforms of 2009. Here's Leonard's response:

Regret   Fulfillment

I would have wagered that Leonard would be bitter about the premature end to his career—and that his bitterness would translate into profound regret. Apparently not. I asked him how he could feel this way, given how young he was and how much more he could have accomplished.

He said, "I'm a lucky man. A statistics professor told me that I had a small gift. I could see rates of change in yields and interest rates in my head. So I went into bond trading, the one field where I could get paid for my small talent. I ended up at a firm with a compensation scheme that was pure pay-for-play. If I made a profit, my share was contractually spelled out to the penny. If I didn't, I was out. I made money every year and I never felt underpaid or cheated. I got exactly what I deserved, and thus it felt fully earned. That's not only satisfying when I look back on it; it's gratifying because I still have the money." He was laughing when he said this, clearly astonished by his good fortune and also delighted.

His rationale disarmed me. For years I had maintained a prejudice about Wall Street types, believing they were smart people who went into the financial sector grudgingly, not because they were fascinated by markets but because it was an easy way to make a pile of money, get out early, and spend the rest of their lives doing what they really wanted to do. They were willing to sacrifice their best years doing something lucrative that they didn't necessarily love so they could achieve independence and comfort at the end. He showed me I was wrong. He loved trading securities. It came easily to him, which increased his chances of being demonstrably excellent at it. The fact that he was in a field that paid very well for excellent performance wasn't a reward as such; it was a means to an end. Fulfillment to him came from the validation of being a star at his job and, as a result, being a good provider for his family. I asked him to grade himself on the six Fulfillers as if I were a doctor conducting an annual physical. Each category was under his control. He had always been aiming for financial security so he could provide for his immediate as well as extended family, which checked off purpose, achievement, and meaning. His engagement had been total, "perhaps excessive," he allowed. He loved trading. His relationships with his wife and grown children were solid. "I'm perpetually amazed my kids still want to spend time with me," he said. Ten years after leaving the trading desk, he was giving away a healthy portion of his fortune and repurposing his professional expertise by providing pro bono financial advice. I didn't bother asking him if he was happy. The answer was written on his face.

Red Hayes, the man who wrote the 1950s country music classic "Satisfied Mind," explained that the idea for the song came from his father-in-law, who one day asked him who he thought the richest man in the world was. Red ventured a few names. His father-in-law said, "You're wrong; it is the man with a satisfied mind."

In Leonard, I realized, I had found a rich man with a satisfied mind—someone who had maximized fulfillment, minimized regret. How does this happen?

THIS IS OUR operative definition of an earned life:

> *We are living an earned life when the choices, risks, and effort we make in each moment align with an overarching purpose in our lives, regardless of the eventual outcome.*

The pesky phrase in that definition is the last one, "regardless of the eventual outcome." It goes against much of what we're taught about goal achievement—setting a target, working hard, earning our reward—in modern society.

Each of us knows deep in our heart when any success, major or minor, is merited and when it's a product of a merciful universe taking pity on us for a moment. And we also know the different emotions each result elicits.

Merited success feels inevitable and just, with a tinge of relief that we weren't cheated out of our win by a last-second calamity.

Unmerited success is all relief and wonder at first, the squidgy guilt of being the beneficiary of dumb luck. It's a cloudy, not wholly gratifying feeling—a sheepish sigh rather than a triumphant fist pump. Which explains why, with the passage of time, we so often revise history in our minds, turning our dumb luck into something we actually earned through the application of skill and hard work. We find ourselves standing on third base and insist we hit a triple, when in fact it was a fielder's error that got us from first to third. We play this revisionist mind game to mask the illegitimacy of our "success," proving again E. B. White's trenchant observation that "luck is not something you can mention in the presence of self-made men."

By contrast, something truly earned makes three simple requirements of us:

- We make our best *choice* supported by the facts and the clarity of our goals. In other words, we know what we want and how far we need to go.
- We accept the *risk* involved.
- We put out maximum *effort*.

The deliverable from this magical brew of choice, risk, and maximal effort is the glorious notion of "an earned reward." It's a perfectly valid term—as far as it goes. An earned reward is the ideal solution to every goal we pursue and every desirable behavior we try to perfect in ourselves. We are said to "earn" an income, and a college degree, and other people's trust. We must earn our physical fitness. We must earn respect; it is not given to us freely. And so on with the long menu of human striving: from a corner office to the affection of our children to a good night's sleep to our reputation and character, all must be earned via choice, risk, and maximal effort. This is why we valorize the merited success; there's something heroic about applying maximum energy, wit, and will to get what we think we want.

But an earned reward, no matter how heroic, does not go far enough for my purposes. It certainly didn't help Gunther, the European CEO, feel fulfilled. His entire career was an unbroken succession of earned rewards—of ever greater goals pursued and achieved. But all those earned rewards occurred at work, not at home. They had no power to prevent him from being overwhelmed with regret about his failed family life. They certainly didn't add up to an earned life. Aarin, as well, did not find satisfaction in her impressive string of achievements. Each big win seems to have left her questioning her motivation and commitment: She could have, and should have, tried harder.

In many cases, the outcomes of our choices, risks, and maximal efforts are not "fair and just." Unless you've led an absurdly charmed life, you know that life is not always fair. It starts at birth: who your parents are, where you grow up, your educational opportunities, and so many other factors, most of them beyond your control. Some of us draw the silver spoon, some the lump of coal. In some cases, the disadvantages we inherit can be overcome through shrewd decisions and maximum effort. Even then, life's inequities can bite, e.g. you're the perfect job candidate but some-body's nephew gets hired instead. You can do everything right, but there's no guarantee the outcome will be just and fair to you. You can be bitter and angry, whining "It isn't fair." Or you can accept life's disappointments with grace. Just don't expect every attempt to "earn" a goal to deliver the appropriate reward. The payoff is not as reliable as you wish or deserve.

There's another, more damning reason I hesitate to put too much faith in the concept of an earned reward—namely, that it's too impermanent and fragile a vessel to contain our wishes and desires for an earned life. The emotional lift we get from an earned reward is fleeting. Happiness leaks out of us from the first second we're aware of it. We get a long-sought promotion, and with alarm-ing haste we raise our sights to the next rung on the ladder, as if we're already dissatisfied with what we worked so hard to earn. We campaign for months to win an election, then, after a quick celebra-tion, immediately have to get to work for the voters. The striving is over; a new striving begins. Whatever prize we have earned—a big raise, a partnership, an ecstatic review—our victory dance is brief. Our sense of fulfillment and happiness simply doesn't last.

I'm not denigrating the value of an earned reward—and all the energy that went into creating it. Setting goals and earning the desired outcomes are essential first steps for success at anything. I'm questioning their utility in achieving an earned life when they are estranged from a greater purpose in our lives.

This is why Leonard the Wall Street trader felt a sense of fulfill-ment in his life where others, perhaps more fortunate and accom-plished than he, fell short. He wasn't in the money game merely to make money. His striving was grounded in the higher purpose of protecting and providing for his family. An earned reward not connected to a higher purpose is a hollow achievement—like a basketball player who's interested only in maintaining his high scoring average rather than making the myriad sacrifices (e.g. taking a charge, diving for loose balls, guarding the opponent's best player) that win close games and championships.

In these pages, we will see that an earned life makes only a few demands of us:

- Live your own life, not someone else's version of it.
- Commit yourself to "earning" every day. Make it a habit.
- Attach your earning moments to something greater than mere personal ambition.

In the end, an earned life doesn't include a trophy ceremony. The reward of living an earned life is being engaged in the process of constantly earning such a life.

THIS BOOK WAS written during the COVID pandemic, while I was isolated with my wife, Lyda, in a one-bedroom rental along the Pacific Ocean in southern California. We had just sold our home of thirty years in Rancho Santa Fe, north of San Diego, and were waiting in the apartment to make a permanent move to Nashville, where our twin grandchildren, Avery and Austin, live. We waited fifteen months to move out.

Unlike my other writing, this book is inspired not only by the lives of my coaching clients, using their examples as source material, but also by my own. It's written at a moment in my life when I still haven't done all I want to do, but I'm running out of time. So I have to make choices. I have to let go of dreams I entertained in my younger days, not solely because the clock is ticking but also because those dreams don't make sense to me anymore.

This book is a reflection on my future. I've learned it's never too late to reflect, because as long as you're breathing, you have more time. But it's never too early either—and early is better. That's what I hope, you the reader, whatever your age, take away from these pages as you reflect on the life you're shaping for yourself and make choices based on that reflection. There is a lot of soul-searching here about people who helped me and what they taught me. There's a lot of soul-searching because of the pandemic, which turned out to be an extraordinary eighteen months of nonmonetary "earning" for me. There's also a lot of soul-searching because I'm at a stage of life when the opportunities to confront existential regret increase predictably—for the simple reason that the ten- or twenty-year intervals into the future that may have dictated my choices in earlier days, when time seemed limitless, are no longer a rational option for me. I may live thirty more years and reach one hundred. But I can't count on that, nor do I know whether my good health will continue or which friends and colleagues will be around to notice. As my time on earth gets shorter, I have to conduct triage with all the unchecked boxes on my life list. Which items are not doable? Which items no longer seem so important? Which two or three items are absolute musts that I'll seriously regret not achieving? I want to use my remaining time to maximize fulfillment and minimize my regrets.

This book is one of my absolute musts. I hope it serves you well, teaching you to use your time providentially and to finish with no regrets.

INTRODUCTORY EXERCISE

What Does "Earned" Mean to You?

Think of a moment in your life that offers the most inarguable connection between what you set out to accomplish and what you ended up with. Perhaps your moment is as simple as wanting an A in algebra and devoting the hours of study to get it. Or maybe it's that time you came up with a brilliant insight that instantly solved a problem that had all your colleagues stumped, elevating their opinion of you. Or maybe it's an achievement with many moving parts: starting up your own business, writing a script and getting it sold, creating a product and bringing it to market. Each of these is an "earned" event, discrete and attached to a specific goal. Hopefully, the feeling of success was sufficiently gratifying that you wanted to repeat it. This is how a life of earned rewards is built, one achieved goal at a time. But the sum is not always greater than the parts. This string of earned rewards doesn't necessarily deliver an earned life.

DO THIS: Now take that earned feeling and amplify it. Connect it to some objective greater than a transitory goal, something worthy of pursuing for the rest of your life. Pick one overarching purpose in your life. Perhaps you want to connect your earned events to a spiritual practice so you can steadily become a more enlightened human being. Or it's something as farsighted as creating a legacy that benefits other people after you're gone. Perhaps it's someone else's example that inspires you to be a better person (e.g. the famous closing scene in *Saving Private Ryan*, in which a dying Captain John Miller, played by Tom Hanks, having sacrificed his life to save Private Ryan, whispers to him, "Earn this"). Your options are endless, but the earning process remains the same: (a) making a choice, (b) accepting the risk, and (c) getting it done with no gas left in the tank. The only difference is that you're attaching your efforts not to a material reward but to an overarching purpose for your life.

Although this is a warm-up exercise before the heavy lifting, it's not an easy one. Most of us, at any age, have rarely been challenged to identify a greater life purpose. Fulfilling the mundane demands of daily life is more than enough to occupy our brain from hour to hour. Remember: This is not a graded test, nor is your answer binding forever (it can change as you change). What matters is your attempt at an answer, however effortless or struggling. Now you're ready to begin.

Part I

CHOOSING
YOUR LIFE

CHAPTER 1

THE "EVERY BREATH" PARADIGM

When Gautama Buddha said, "Every breath I take is a new me," he wasn't speaking metaphorically. He meant it literally.

Buddha was teaching that life is a progression of discrete moments of constant reincarnation from a previous you to a present you. At one moment, through your choices and actions, you may experience pleasure, happiness, sadness, or fear. But that specific emotion doesn't linger. With each breath, it alters, eventually vanishing. It was experienced by a previous you. Whatever you hope will happen in your next breath, or the next day, or the next year will be experienced by a different you, the future you. The only iteration of you that matters is the present you who has just taken a breath.

I start with the assumption that Buddha was right.

That doesn't mean you have to abandon your articles of spiritual faith or convert to Buddhism.* I'm only asking you to consider

---

*I came to Buddhism when I was nineteen years old, not because I was looking to be converted to a new theology but because it articulated ideas that were forming fuzzily in my curious teenage brain. I came to Buddhism for confirmation and clarity, not conversion. The Every Breath Paradigm (my name for it, not Buddha's) took hold after years of study. Discussing it in my work with clients came later, when my Western training failed to work

Buddha's insight as a new paradigm for thinking about your relationship to the passage of time and living an earned life.

A core pillar of Buddhism is *impermanence*—the notion that the emotions, thoughts, and material possessions we hold now do not last. They can vanish in an instant—as brief as the time we need to take our next breath. We know this to be empirically true. Our discipline, motivation, our good humor—you name it—they do not last. They fall out of our grasp as suddenly as they appeared.

Nevertheless, we have a hard time accepting impermanence as a rational way to understand our life, that the unity and singleness of our identity and character is an illusion. The Western paradigm, so deeply ingrained since childhood, is an ongoing argument against impermanence. Actually, it is a fairy tale, always with the same ending: *And then they lived happily ever after.* The Western paradigm is all about endeavoring for something better in the future and believing two things will result: (a) *whatever our improvement, we remain essentially the same person we have been (only better),* and (b) *against all the evidence, this time it will last.* It will be a permanent solution to whatever's gnawing away at our spirit. That makes about as much sense as studying hard for an A in math and thinking it will make you an A student forever, or believing that

---

with behaviorally challenged bosses in the workplace. Steeped in the Western paradigm, they clung to their past triumphs as proof that they did not need to change their behavior to produce more triumphs. "If I'm so bad, how come I'm so successful?" they'd argue, ignoring the possibility that they were successful despite their faults, not because of them. Getting them to distinguish between their past and present selves via Buddha's teaching was my Hail Mary pass to ensure that their next triumph was behavioral, not technical or intellectual.

your personality is fixed and you can never change, or that rising housing prices will never go down.

This is the Great Western Disease of "I'll be happy when . . ." It is the pervasive mindset whereby we convince ourselves that we'll be happy when we get that promotion, or drive a Tesla, or finish a slice of pizza, or attain any other badge of our short- or long-term desires. Of course, when the badge is finally in our hands, something comes along that compels us to discount the badge's value and renew our striving for the next badge. And the next. We want to reach the next level in the organizational hierarchy. We want a Tesla with more range. We order another pizza slice to go. We are living in what Buddha called the realm of the "hungry ghost," always eating but never satisfied.

This is a frustrating way to live, which is why I'm urging a different way of seeing the world—one that venerates the present moment rather than the moment before or after.

When I explain the Every Breath Paradigm to clients, accustomed as they are to goal setting and high achievement, it takes a while for them to accept the primacy of now over the validating pleasures of remembering past successes or the future-facing buzz of pursuing an ambitious goal. Being forward-looking is second nature to them, as is looking backward to take pride in their track record. The present moment, astonishingly, is almost a secondary thought.

Gradually I chip away at their attitude. When clients beat themselves up over a blunder, recent or ancient, I say "Stop" and ask them to repeat the following: "That was a previous me. The present me didn't make that blunder. So why am I torturing myself for some past error that the present version of me didn't commit?"

Then I have them make the universal hand gesture for shaking off a problem and repeat after me: "Let it go." Silly as this routine may sound, it works. Clients not only begin to see the futility of belaboring the past, but they also embrace the psychically soothing notion that the blunder was committed by someone else—a previous self. They can forgive that previous self and move on. In my initial meetings with clients, I may employ this routine a half dozen times in a one-hour conversation. But eventually they get it—usually at a critical or fraught moment when they finally appreciate that the Every Breath Paradigm has utility in their daily life, not just in their career.

TEN YEARS AGO I began coaching an executive in his early forties who had been tapped to be the next CEO of a media company. Let's call him Mike. His natural leadership skills set him apart from the standard C-suite issue of smart, motivated, underpromise-and-overdeliver types. But he had some rough edges that needed smoothing, which is where I came in.

Mike was a charmer when it served his interests, but he could be insensitive and dismissive to people less useful to him. He was super-persuasive, but sometimes aggressive when people didn't immediately concede he was right and they were wrong. He was also visibly too pleased with his success, which bathed him in an annoying scent of entitlement. He was special and never let people forget it.

Insensitive, rarely wrong, and entitled. These weren't career-killing flaws, just issues that came up in my 360-degree reviews with his colleagues and direct reports, which I shared with him. He accepted the criticism with grace, and in less than two years (through a process that is the essence of one-on-one coaching) changed his behavior to his own satisfaction and, more important, in the opinion of his peers. (You need to change a lot to get people to notice even a little.) We remained friends after he became CEO, talking at least once a month about his job and, increasingly, about his family life. He and his wife—college sweethearts—had four grown kids, all out of the house and on their own. The marriage was solid after years of tension when Mike was focused on his career while his wife, Sherry, raised the kids and built up a seemingly unshakable resentment of Mike's self-absorption and insensitivity.

"Is Sherry wrong?" I asked, pointing out that if he had been perceived as insensitive and entitled at work, he probably was the same at home.

"But I've changed," he said. "She's even admitted it. And we're much happier. Why won't she let it go?"

I explained the Every Breath Paradigm to him, stressing how hard it was for Westerners to conceive that we are not a unitary mass of flesh and bone and emotions and memories but rather a steadily expanding multitude of individuals, each one time-stamped in the moment of our most recent breath—and reborn with every breath.

I told Mike, "When your wife thinks about her marriage, she can't separate the previous Mike from the man who is her husband today. They're one character to her, a permanent persona. It's how we all think if we're not careful."

Mike struggled with the concept. It would come up from time to time in our talks, but he couldn't think of himself as a running series of many Mikes, a new one nearly eight million times a year (the estimated number of breaths we take annually). It collided with his fixed self-image of the impressive, successful Mike that he projected to the world. I couldn't fault him for that. I was offering him a new paradigm, not a casual suggestion. We achieve under-standing at our own pace.

We still talk regularly and he's still a CEO. But in the summer of 2019 he called me out of the blue, excitedly announcing, "I got it!" I had no idea what he was talking about, but it soon became clear the "it" was about our Every Breath talks. He described a con-versation he'd had the day before with Sherry. They were driving back from a Fourth of July reunion at their weekend home with the kids and their partners and friends. It was a crowded but joyous weekend, and Mike and Sherry were reliving the high points on the two-hour drive, pleased at how the children turned out, how engaging and helpful their friends were, how the kids did most of the cooking and cleaning up. Basically, they were congratulating themselves on their good fortune and their successful parenting. Then Sherry threw a wet blanket on their reverie.

"I just wish you had contributed more when they were growing up," she said. "I was so alone most of the time."

"I wasn't hurt by her words, or angry," Mike told me. "I turned to her and very calmly said, 'You're right about that guy ten years ago. He was clueless about many things. But that's not the guy in this car right now. He's a better man now. Tomorrow he's going to be someone else trying to be a little better. Another thing—that woman who suffered back then is not the same woman today. You're faulting me for the actions of someone who doesn't exist anymore. It's not right.'"

The car was silent for a long ten seconds. Then Sherry apolo-gized, adding, "You're right. I have to work on that."

Mike had required years—and an emotionally heightened situation to which Buddha's teaching applied perfectly—to under-stand the Every Breath Paradigm. His wife got it in ten seconds.

I'm okay with both timetables, always glad to be an accomplice in other people's epiphanies.

IMPERMANENCE IS EASY to accept if you're in the business of helping people change. I wouldn't have purpose or a career without it. When you accept that everything that flourishes also decays and disappears, you're accepting a viewpoint that doesn't apply only to worldly achievements and status. It applies powerfully to your personal development as well. You see that the person you have been is not a life sentence to remain that person today or in the future. You can let past transgressions go—and move on.

Okay, you say. Enough with the feathery quasispirituality, Marshall. How does this Every Breath Paradigm connect to living an earned life?

The connection is as immediate and direct as flipping a switch to fill a dark room with light. If we accept that everything of value that we have earned—from the small stuff like a teacher's praise to the big stuff like our good reputation or the reciprocated love of the people we love—is impermanent, subject to the whims and indifference of the world, we must also accept that these prized "possessions" need to be constantly re-earned, practically on a daily or hourly basis, perhaps as frequently as with every breath.

Reminding clients to stop torturing themselves about their past failures ("That was a previous you. Time to let it go") may be one of my more valuable contributions to them. But equally valuable, I think, is when the opposite occurs: when clients feel the need to replay their career highlight reel for me. I see this most vividly in former athletes and CEOs who are struggling to create their next life. When they talk nostalgically about previous triumphs, whether it's winning a gold medal fifteen years ago or leading an organization of twenty thousand people six months earlier, it's my duty to yank them back to the present, reminding them that they are not that admired athlete or commanding CEO anymore. That was someone else. It's no different from preferring to live vicariously through someone famous whom you follow religiously on social media. That famous person doesn't know or care that you exist; you are strangers to each other. Likewise with your constant returning to the glories of a previous you. It's not that the honors and attention and respect, each well earned in its time, were never real. But they have faded. To recall them is no longer an expression of fulfillment; it's actually a moan of regret about their impermanence, about how swiftly and unceremoniously they slipped away.

Recapturing that sense of fulfillment cannot be accomplished by wallowing in memories of who we were and what we accomplished. It can be earned only by the person we are in the moment at hand. And earned again and again in subsequent moments when we are someone new again. As the basketball coach Phil Jackson, a student of Buddhism, said after winning two consecutive NBA championships in the mid-1990s with the Chicago Bulls and then going for a third ring in 1998, "You're only a success in the moment of the successful act. Then you have to do it again."

The truth is, we are never finished earning our life. There is no hard-stop moment when we can tell ourselves, "I've earned enough. I'm done." We might as well stop breathing.

EXERCISE

The Two Letters

This exercise is for people who intellectually understand the Every Breath Paradigm but haven't developed the muscle memory that makes it natural and instinctive in their lives. They aren't yet capable of creating a psychological wall between their previous and current selves so that the distinction is their new credo. They still believe that there is some unseen and untouchable part of their being that is fixed and immutable—their essence, spirit, or soul—and defines who they are. When they confuse their previous and current selves, thinking of the two interchangeably, the Two Letters Exercise never fails to unmuddle them. One letter is about gratitude, the other is about investing in the future.

Letter One: First, write a letter to a previous you expressing gratitude for that previous self's specific act of creativity or hard work or discipline—preferably something earned rather than given—that has made you better today in some way. It can be recent or long ago. The only criterion is that you single out this action as a difference maker in your life now. I've done this thank-a-previous-you exercise many times with people. One man thanked the previous him who turned vegan eight years earlier for the good health and vigor he feels today. One writer thanked her ten-year-old self for adopting the dictionary habit of looking up every unfamiliar word she read and entering it in a small notebook all through middle school and on up to grad school. "No notebook," she said, "no writing life." One woman thanked her six-year-old self for learning to swim because it had saved her life on at least two occasions.

Another thanked his eighteen-year-old self for choosing the college where he met his wife.

The exercise not only creates separation between you then and you now, but it reveals a cause-and-effect link between past and present that you might fail to make as memory fades. In your most grateful and humble moments, you may have uttered the cliché "I stand on the shoulders of giants." This letter helps identify a giant you may have forgotten—the previous you.

Take a deep breath. Think of all the previous gifts that the previous you has given to the you that is reading this sentence. If any group of people gave you so many wonderful gifts, what would you say to these nice people? This is your chance to say "Thank you."

Letter Two: Now write a letter from the present you to a future you, one year, five years, ten years down the road. Spell out the investment—in the currency of sacrifice, effort, education, relationships, discipline—that you are making now to benefit the person the letter is addressed to. The investment could be in any form of self-development—from improving your health to getting a graduate degree to putting a percentage of every paycheck into Treasury bills. Think of it as an act of philanthropy, except you do not actually know the beneficiary. Not yet.

I got the idea from the great NFL running back Curtis Martin. Curtis was living the Every Breath Paradigm years before we met. He stumbled reluctantly into football, not playing until his junior year in high school, when a coach convinced him that joining the team would take him away for three hours a day from the life-threatening streets of his Pittsburgh neighborhood. He'd once been mistaken for someone else and had a gun put in his face—the trigger was pulled, but the bullet jammed. By his senior year, every major college program was recruiting him. He chose nearby

Pitt. Despite an injury-riddled college career, there were enough flashes of talent that the New England Patriots drafted him in the third round in 1995. Whereas most young athletes regard Draft Day as winning the lottery, Curtis's first thought was "I don't want to do this." A pastor persuaded Curtis to stick with football, showing him how the NFL could be a vehicle for creating the rest of his life, which Curtis wanted to be a life of service to others. That's the mental picture that gave Curtis purpose and motivation. He would play football as an investment in his post-NFL self. That's not the usual motivating force for elite athletes. They love to compete. They're obsessed with winning now; the future will take care of itself. But Curtis was playing a longer game. He retired as the fourth leading rusher in NFL history (behind Emmitt Smith, Walter Payton, and Barry Sanders) after a career-ending injury in his eleventh NFL season. During his playing days he had founded the Curtis Martin Job Foundation, which supports single mothers, disabled people, and at-risk youth. On his first day as a former football player, Curtis was ready and eager to shake hands with the future he had invested in twelve years earlier. He was living his new life.*

Curtis Martin's story is a positive example of investing in a future you. Gunther, the regret-filled CEO introduced earlier, is a negative example. Gunther worked his entire life to make enough money so that his three children wouldn't have to work as hard as he did. It was a monumental error. The children were neither grateful nor productive because of the money, which they used

---

* Curtis explained all of this in his speech at his induction into the NFL Hall of Fame in 2012. It is generally acknowledged as one of the most candid and powerful speeches in the event's history. It is the model for your letter to your future self.

as a license to do nothing. His error: He wasn't investing in his future self or his legacy as a father. He was merely making a gift. The difference is profound. An investment comes with an anticipated return. A gift comes with no strings attached. He had given his children a gift that they neither earned nor deserved, hoping for but never articulating what he expected in return from them. In the end he had neither their gratitude for his sacrifice nor the fulfillment of seeing them create productive lives of their own. He likened his regret to the explosive ending of *The Bridge on the River Kwai*, when the British prisoner of war Colonel Nicholson discovers that Allied soldiers have dynamite-rigged the bridge he has built for the Japanese to help his troops maintain morale during captivity and in which he has come to feel such a misplaced pride of achievement that he at first tries to sabotage the attempt to destroy it. At last realizing his folly, he says, "What have I done?"— then falls on the plunger to destroy the bridge himself.

If Gunther had written a letter to his future self, his children's lives might have turned out differently. The second letter is more than an exercise in writing down your goals. It forces you to regard your well-intentioned efforts today as an investment in the people you are most responsible for raising into productive, happy human beings: yourself and those you love most. It is not a gift; you're expecting a return.

CHAPTER 2

WHAT'S STOPPING YOU FROM CREATING YOUR OWN LIFE?

In the early 2000s I started spending eight days a year teaching leadership courses to Goldman Sachs executives and their top clients. My liaison at the powerful Wall Street firm was Mark Tercek, a partner in his forties who oversaw Goldman's training programs as well as their investments in the education sector. Mark was a quintessential Wall Street type: smart, charismatic, high-energy, and keenly focused on putting money to work for the firm. But he was also modest, self-effacing, and intimidatingly well rounded. He practiced yoga, was a strict vegan, competed in triathlons, and was an ardent environmentalist. In 2005, he was tapped to create and manage the firm's environmental markets group. Three years later, because of Mark's deep connections in the field, a friend at an executive search firm called him to suggest candidates for the CEO spot at the Nature Conservancy, the largest environmental nonprofit in the United States. As Mark thought about other names and their qualifications, an unexpected notion popped into his head: *What about me?* He was perfectly suited for the job. The Nature Conservancy is essentially a philanthropic "bank," spending its endowment and annual contributions to buy vast tracts of nature in need of protection. Financial discipline, his expertise, was a major qualification. Plus, in his heart, he really wanted it. His wife, Amy, an equally committed environmentalist, supported the move.

Mark and I had developed a bond of trust by this time, so I invited him to my home in Rancho Santa Fe where we could spend a couple of days away from the corporate noise to consider next moves. Should he end a consequential career at Goldman and uproot his four kids from New York to Washington, D.C., to run a nonprofit? The more we talked, the clearer it was that the pluses overwhelmed the minuses. Yet Mark still hesitated. Near the end of our time together, a few hours before his flight back to New York, he was still in limbo. So I took him for a long trek through the woods and bridle paths in our neighborhood. I'd done this often with clients; getting lost in nature clears the mind.

At some point, as he remained indecisive without a convincing reason, I asked him, "Why can't you pull the trigger? It's not an offer. It's just an interview."

"If I get the job, I'm afraid of what my Goldman partners will think," he said.

I was incredulous. We had spent hours reviewing his career, his skill set, his intellectual interests, his wins and his disappointments. He'd given his entire adult life—twenty-four years—to the firm. He was perfect for the new job, plus he could afford the pay cut (the Goldman IPO nine years earlier had guaranteed his financial security). He had no excuses not to try for the position, and yet *this* was what was holding him back—the absurd fear that his colleagues would think he was giving up, that he wasn't tough enough to endure the rigors of Wall Street?

I grabbed his arm to stop him on the trail and face him directly. I wanted him to focus on the words that were about to come out of my mouth:

"Dammit, Mark. When are you going to start living your own life?"

I'd been advising executives for years on the proper timing for leaving a big job—and I'd heard all the excuses for staying, mostly variations on three themes:

- The indispensability argument: *The organization needs me.*
- The winner's argument: *We're on a hot streak. It's too soon to quit.*
- The no-place-to-go argument: *I have no idea what I want to do next.*

But I'd never heard someone at Mark's level give up on a dream because of what his peers would think. My outburst must have hit home, because Mark called the search team leader the next day to nominate himself, and shortly thereafter he left Goldman to become CEO of the Nature Conservancy. That moment with Mark is *the* instigative event for this book and the concept of an "earned life," although I didn't know it at the time.

Ten years later, after his tenure at the Nature Conservancy had become a big success, Mark reminded me of our one-sided shouting match. My words—*Dammit, when are you going to start living your own life?*—remained etched in his brain, functioning as a kind of mnemonic device reminding him to stay true to the things that give his life meaning and purpose. Being a good husband and father. Making a contribution. Saving the planet. (You know, the small stuff.)

Frankly, I'd forgotten that moment on the trail, but his call swept me back to his side of the argument that day, specifically his bewildering fear of what his peers would think of him. I couldn't understand how Mark's fear of others' opinions almost froze him from trying to land the TNC job, a choice that would have flooded him with regret. (We don't feel regret because we tried and failed; we regret not trying.)

After I hung up with Mark, another memory hit me. I recalled my friend, the late Dr. Roosevelt Thomas, Jr., a Harvard Ph.D. in organizational behavior, who reshaped corporate America's attitudes about workplace diversity. One of Roosevelt's crucial insights was the unappreciated influence of *referent groups* in everyday life. Early in my career we co-wrote a paper on the subject, although only he went on to make it part of his life's work.

Each of us, Roosevelt Thomas contended, feels emotionally and intellectually connected to a specific cohort of the population. We think of this concept as "tribalism" today, but in the early 1970s, the idea of referent groups to explain social upheaval and the differences among people was a breakthrough concept. A referent group could be vast, like the community of a specific religion or political party, or it could be as small as, say, the people who love the band Phish (aka Phish-heads). It would be impossible to catalog all the referent groups in the United States. They are more numerous than Twitter hashtags, and they procreate like rabbits. Roosevelt Thomas's point was that if you know a person's referent group—to whom or what they feel deeply connected, whom they want to impress, whose respect they crave—you can understand why they talk and think and behave the way they do. (The corollary here is that most of us also have a *counter-referent group*. We base our allegiance and choices on what we oppose rather than what we support, whether it's Democrat vs. Republican or Real Madrid vs. Barcelona. What we abhor shapes us almost as much as what we love.) You don't have to agree with people in other referent groups, but if you appreciate the influence exerted by such groups, you are less likely to be stupefied by their adherents' choices or dismiss them as "idiots."*

I saw how Roosevelt Thomas's theory applied to Mark. I had the false impression that Mark's referent group comprised socially concerned people who were vegan, practiced yoga, and cared about the environment—just like him. The truth was that after twenty-four years, Mark was still emotionally linked to his aggressive, bespoke-suit-wearing, deal-making colleagues at Goldman Sachs. Their approval still mattered to him. Expecting Mark to instantly abandon this referent group was a big ask, akin to demanding that he deny his identity. It was so powerful that he was willing to sacrifice the gift that fell into his lap with the search firm's initial call, namely, the opportunity to re-create his own life.

Mark's call triggered an insight. Although I was gratified that my exhortation to "start living your own life" proved to be a persuasive phrase for him, the teacher in me wondered: *If someone as driven and accustomed to success as Mark could be thwarted by his referent group, how many other people, many with fewer resources and opportunities, were being equally blocked for wholly different reasons?* What were the forces stopping them from creating their own lives? And what could I do to help?

The good news is that it is easier to create your own life today than it has ever been in human history. In the past, almost all of

---

*For the record, teachers are my referent group. My mother was a teacher, and she was my biggest influence growing up. Thus, I identify with teachers. I judge myself on my ability to impart what I know to help others. The respect I value most comes from teachers. That said, this personal fact is hidden, rarely revealed or openly discussed. Even lifelong friends might not know this about me unless I told them. That's how mysterious a person's referent group can be. You have to probe hard to figure it out. Your reward, though, is an eye-opening recalibration and understanding of someone you only thought you knew.

us were second-class citizens from birth. We could not vote and choose our leaders. Conformity was the rule and any difference was punished, whether that difference was whom we loved or which deity we worshipped (if in fact we worshipped any deity). We may have had more sorrow, but we had less regret. You cannot regret your decisions if you're not allowed to make decisions.

The trend line of the last hundred years suggests that we will continue acquiring more rights and more freedoms. In much of the world, we are no longer serfs, women can vote, hundreds of millions of people are rising out of poverty, and it's okay to be gay. In other words, many of us have reason to be optimistic. The icing on this layer cake of optimism is technology: In expanding our mobility and access to information, technology has multiplied the number of choices beckoning us. More freedom, more movement, more options in work and play.

That's a problem—and I'm hardly the only one making this big claim. One of Peter Drucker's valedictory insights before he died at age ninety-five in 2005 said as much:

In a few hundred years, when the history of our time will be written from a long-term perspective, it is likely that the most important event historians will see is not technology, not the Internet, not e-commerce. It is an unprecedented change in the human condition. For the first time— literally—substantial and rapidly growing numbers of people have choices. For the first time, they will have to manage themselves. And society is totally unprepared for it.*

* Peter F. Drucker, "Managing Knowledge Means Managing Oneself," *Leader to Leader* 16 (Spring 2000): 8–10.

Freedom and mobility create what Barry Schwartz famously described as "the paradox of choice." We do better with fewer choices, not more. Faced with thirty-nine flavors of ice cream, we often make a disappointing choice. It's much easier to pick between two options—say, vanilla or mint chocolate chip—and be satisfied. It's the same with creating your own life in a complex, rapidly advancing world: Not only is it hard to sift through the myriad choices, but even when we know what we want, we don't always know how to follow our dreams.

The barriers holding us back in our choices and actions, frustrating our will to live our own life, are formidable and numerous, beginning with these:

1. OUR FIRST OPTION, UNFORTUNATELY, IS INERTIA

Inertia is the most resolute and determinative opponent of change. For years, whenever I've been confronted with clients failing at changing the behavior they insist they want to change, I have fallen back on the following mantra: *Our default response in life is not to experience meaning or happiness. Our default response is to experience inertia.* I want them not only to appreciate inertia's omnipresence but to see *their* particular inertia in a new light.

We think of inertia as the state of being inert or motionless—one of our purer displays of passivity and disengagement. It's not. Inertia is an active event in which we are *persisting* in the state we're already in rather than switching to something else. This is not mere semantics. It's a different point of view, characterizing even our most sloth-like passivity as the active choice to persist in the status quo (i.e., no choice is a choice too; it's choosing to say "I'll pass"). On the other hand, the moment we shift into a new gear and choose to engage in something different, we cease to persist as inertia's patsy. Being inertia's victim or escaping its malign gravitational pull is a choice that's solely ours to make. When people discover that they have a choice, they are usually empowered to change.

Another intriguing characteristic of inertia is how well it provides us with a glimpse of our short-term future. It is more accurate than any algorithm or forecasting model. Inertia is the reason I can stipulate the following rule about your immediate future: *The most reliable predictor of what you'll be doing five minutes from now is what you're doing now.* If you're taking a nap or cleaning your home or shopping online, there's a high probability that you'll be doing the same thing five minutes from now. This short-term principle also applies in the long term. The most reliable predictor of who you'll be five years from now is who you are now. If you don't know a foreign language now or how to make bread from scratch, you probably won't know in five years either. If you're not talking to your estranged father now, chances are you won't be talking to him five years from now. And so on for most of the details that describe your life today.

Appreciating our agency over inertia's impact teaches us how to shape it into a positive force. When we develop productive (rather than destructive) habits or routines—e.g. exercising first thing in the morning, eating the same nutritious breakfast, taking the same hyperefficient route to work each day—inertia is our friend, keeping us grounded and committed and consistent.

These are the features that make inertia a major force affecting every aspect of an earned life. But even when we gain dominion over inertia, there remain a few other targeted forces that also block us from living our own life.

2. OUR PROGRAMMING LOCKS US IN PLACE

I grew up in Valley Station, Kentucky, thirty miles south of Lou-
isville, along the section of the Ohio River that forms the Indiana border. I was my mother's only child and she devoted herself
to shaping my childhood persona and self-image. She was an elementary school teacher who valued brain over brawn. She programmed me to believe that I was the sharpest kid in town. In
addition, perhaps to prevent me from becoming an auto mechanic
or electrician or any other kind of skilled craftsman, she regularly
reminded me that I had no eye-hand coordination or mechanical
skills. Thus, by middle school, I had a talent for math and for acing
standardized tests, but I was terrible at anything mechanical or
athletic. I couldn't change a lightbulb, and the one time in Little
League that I actually made contact between ball and bat—it was a
foul ball—I received a standing ovation.

Fortunately, I responded to my mother's programming with an
unshakable faith in my intelligence. Unfortunately, I also developed an unpardonable self-assurance that I didn't need to try very
hard at school. I learned that I could coast and still pull down decent grades. This lucky streak continued through college at Rose-
Hulman Institute of Technology and the MBA program at Indiana
University—and emboldened me (despite my years of suboptimal
effort for academic studies) to seek a Ph.D. at UCLA. I could not
articulate why I needed a doctorate in organizational behavior or
what I would do with it. Coasting had gotten me this far, I rea-
soned. Why not see where continued coasting could take me? At
UCLA, I was blessed with classmates who were my intellectual superiors and professors who were not only light-years smarter but
also intimidating presences who were not shy about humiliating

me for my vanities and hypocrisies. It was a necessary comeup-
pance. I was twenty-six years old and finally learning that I was at
UCLA to *earn* a Ph.D., not merely receive it. I needed that many
years to overcome the unintended consequences of my mother's
programming.

All of us are programmed in some way by our parents. Mom and
Dad can't help it (and it's usually well-meaning). They shape our
beliefs, our social values, how we treat other people, how we behave
in a relationship, even which sports teams we cheer for. More than
anything else, they program our self-image. From our early days
in the crib—before we can crawl, walk, or speak—they're forensi-
cally studying our behavior for clues about our talents and potential. This is most obvious when siblings are involved. Over time,
with enough "evidence," our parents subdivide us into distinct personalities: the smart one, pretty one, strong one, nice one, responsible one—whichever of the many descriptors seems to apply at the
time. It's as if they're unwittingly trying to turn us into an archetype
of a human being, erasing all the nuance. If we're not careful, we
not only accept the programming but adapt our behavior to it. The
smart one falls back on cleverness rather than expertise, the pretty
one relies on her looks, the strong one prefers raw power to persuasion, the nice one acquiesces too quickly, the responsible one sacrifices too much in the name of duty. Whose life are we living when
decisive parts of it, imprinted during our formative years by people
we love, have already been created for us?

The good news is that we have the right to deprogram ourselves
whenever we want. Our programming is only a problem when
it becomes a life blocker. We consider trying something new—
a U-turn in our career, a new haircut—then reject it with excuses
such as "I've never been good at _____" or "It's not me." Until

we (or someone else) challenge the validity of our excuses ("Says who?"), we cannot imagine imposing our will upon beliefs that we've come to accept as gospel. Our programming's biggest impact is how proficiently it blinds us to our need to reject it.

3. WE ARE UNDONE BY OBLIGATION

You might be familiar with a poignant scene in the 1989 Ron Howard film, *Parenthood,* starring Steve Martin as Gil Buckman, beleaguered father of three, and Mary Steenburgen as his serenely accepting wife, Karen. Late in the movie, after we learn that their oldest child, Kevin, has emotional issues and that Gil has just quit a job he hates, Karen informs Gil that she is unexpectedly pregnant with their fourth child. In the middle of a tense conversation about their new situation, Gil starts to leave to coach his son's Little League team "into last place." Karen asks, "Do you really have to go?" Halfway out the door Gil turns back to her with a crazed look and spits out, *"My whole life is 'have to.'"*

The beauty of obligation is that it directs us to keep our promises to others, implied or explicit. The misery of obligation is how often those promises conflict with the ones we've made to ourselves. In those moments, we tend to overcorrect, choosing between the extremes of selfless and selfish—and end up disappointing either ourselves or those who depend on us. Obligation forces us to prioritize our responsibilities. It is a gray area, with few norms to guide us beyond the Golden Rule and "do the right thing." In my experience, there are no rules for dealing with obligation; each situation is different.

Sometimes it's proper and noble to be selfless. We join the family business instead of pursuing a more exciting career. We stay at a dull or hateful job for the paycheck that covers the family bills. We turn down the career-making job in another city because we don't want to uproot the family. There's fulfillment in honoring our obligations to our loved ones.

That said, sometimes it's okay to put ourselves first, in spite of what others think. Such sacrifices and compromises can be agonizing and costly. They're not easily made, but they are honorable and essential too. As the great journalist Herbert Bayard Swope (winner of the first Pulitzer Prize for Reporting in 1917) said, "I can't give you a surefire formula for success. But I can give you a formula for failure: Try to please everybody all the time."

4. WE SUFFER FROM A FAILURE OF IMAGINATION

Choosing between two or three valid ideas for the life you want to lead is a legitimate source of confusion for many people. On the other hand, some people cannot imagine one path for themselves, let alone two or three.

I used to think creativity was a matter of taking two slightly dissimilar ideas and merging them into something original, e.g. serving lobster with steak and calling it Surf 'n' Turf. You add A and B and come up with D. Then a successful artist told me I was setting the bar too low. Creativity is more like taking A and F and L and coming up with Z. The greater the distance between the parts, the greater the imagination required to make them whole. Only a precious few of us are A-plus-F-plus-L-equals-Z creative. Some of us are A-plus-B-equals-D creative. And, sadly, some of us can't even imagine a world where A and B are in the same room.

Reading this book is proof that you're curious about self-improvement. Curiosity is how we prepare to fire up our imagination and picture something new.

If you're among the 30 percent of Americans who have a college degree, you already know from your teenage years what it feels like to seek an identity reboot, a new presentation of self that will improve your odds of earning your place in the world. You already know how to imagine a fresh start. The Pulitzer Prize–winning novelist Richard Russo, author of *Empire Falls,* remembering his undergraduate years, wrote, "College, after all, is where we go to reinvent ourselves, to sever our ties with the past, to become the person we always wanted to be and were prevented from being by people who knew better." Russo compared college to "entering the witness-protection program. You're *supposed* to try on a new identity or two. Indeed, it would not only defeat the purpose, it would be downright dangerous to leave the program easily recognizable as the person who'd entered it."

Think back to your senior year in high school. I'd venture to say that applying to college is the first time you felt control over your future. Although the process is rigidly shaped by a cartel of guidance counselors, testing companies, and college admissions officers (not to mention your parents), at eighteen you were nonetheless running the show. You assessed your strengths and weaknesses. You answered basic questions to set the criteria for the schools: distance, size, prestige, selectivity, social life, climate, cost, financial aid, and other factors. You chose how many schools to apply to. You wrote the essays and secured the recommendations. Then you waited for a decision. If your third or fourth choice college offered significantly better financial aid than your top choice, you adapted, either by solving the cost issue (taking out loans and

working your way through college) or settling for the less appealing school and taking the money.*

Then you matriculated and discovered that whether you were the
prom queen or class clown in high school, the socialite or brainy
geek, college was your opportunity to delete your adolescence and
write a new script. As Russo suggests, you could accurately measure
the success or failure of your college years by how recognizable you
were at graduation compared to the person who had entered the
scene four years earlier. You did it once; you can do it again.

5. WE ARE WINDED BY THE PACE OF CHANGE

If making big claims about society was part of my job description
(it isn't), here's the one claim—learned from Rob Nail of Singular-
ity University—I'd make with confidence:

> *The pace of change you are experiencing today is the slowest pace
> of change you will ever experience for the rest of your life.*

In other words, slow is today, fast is tomorrow. You're delud-
ing yourself in pointless nostalgia if you think that, no matter
the situation, at some point in the near future—when you finish
the "rush" project or when the kids get older and your domestic
life calms down—you can revert to a slower time when the pace

---

*Worst case, if disaster struck and you were shut out by all your top choices
except your safety school, you learned how quickly you can accept and make
peace with the "tragedy" of being offered only one choice. It is a lesson in taking lemons and making lemonade and your introduction to the agency that
comes from having no choice. We'll take a closer look at that in chapter 4.

of life and the speed at which it changed was more relaxed and gentle. It is not going to happen. You and your workmates won't immediately chill out when you finish the rush project. Another emergency job will appear (count on it) and you'll learn that "rush pace" is your new normal. The same with your hectic domestic life; it won't calm down when the kids get older or leave the nest. It's a wheel that won't stop turning. There's always something that needs to be dealt with right away.

Some years ago I hailed a taxi in Manhattan to take me to the airport. The driver drove slowly through midtown traffic, never exceeding 20 mph. He accelerated to a racier 35 mph once we got on the 55 mph roads outside the city. When I asked him if he could go faster, he declined: "This is how fast I drive," he said. "If you like, I'll stop and let you out now." It was as if he had learned to drive in a different time, never noticing that cars had become peppier, roads were better, and passengers were in a hurry.

Our failure to adapt to the quickening pace of change blocks us in the same ways that a failure of imagination does. We cannot interpret what's happening around us. If we cannot keep up, we get winded and fall behind. And when we fall behind, we are living in everyone else's past.

6. WE ARE NARCOTIZED BY VICARIOUS LIVING

When I challenged Mark Tercek to start living his own life, I could easily have asked, "Why are you living someone else's life?" They're really two sides of the same coin known as *vicarious living*. This is the most alarming soul-leeching development I've observed in the last twenty years. Because of social media and a smorgasbord of technological distractions, we have an abundance of opportunities to live through other people's lives rather than live our own. We allow ourselves to be impressed by strangers' social media posturings. Sometimes we return the favor by posturing to impress them, ignoring the likelihood that they're not paying attention to us as avidly as we pay attention to them. In one of vicarious living's more absurd incarnations, we have graduated from playing video games ourselves (itself a simulation of real life) to paying money to watch elite game players compete against one another in our favorite video games. We have gone from watching to watching others do our watching.

Narcotized by technology, we sacrifice long-term purpose and fulfillment for the short-term dopamine-driven feedback loops created by Facebook and Twitter and Instagram. This is not healthy. As with the pace of change, I don't see a horizon where this societal problem slows down because a majority of us suddenly stop using social media's irresistible tools. Only we can control how profoundly we allow vicarious living to infect our life, one individual at a time.

The damage from this trend toward vicarious living is one of heightened distraction. Instead of focusing on what we know we should be doing, we are, in T. S. Eliot's immortal phrasing, "distracted from distraction by distraction." It's not just social media's fault. Our entire world operates as a distraction engine. A warm sunny day, a baseball game on TV, breaking news on the radio, a phone call, a knock at the door, a family emergency, a sudden craving for a doughnut. Anyone or anything can pull our focus from doing what we should be doing and coax us into doing what others want us to do. That's one definition of not living your own life.

7. WE HAVE RUN OUT OF RUNWAY

A friend told me the story of a man named Joe who wanted to be a playwright but discovered in his midtwenties that his true passion was wine. So Joe switched gears and became a wine writer; he would get paid to taste and learn about wine by writing about it. A portion of every writing fee went to buying wine for himself. He was starting out in the late 1970s, long before the world's great wines were priced upward for billionaires. With this head start, on his modest journalist's salary he amassed a fifteen-thousand-bottle collection that was the envy of the wine world. He was generous, not miserly, with his rare wines. If you invited Joe and his wife to your home for dinner, he'd offer to provide the wine—and you'd be a fool to say no. The great winemakers knew him and included him on the short list of connoisseurs who got first crack every year at their limited supply of new vintages. The day came in his mid-sixties when Joe received the annual prerelease offering from one of Italy's superstars, Angelo Gaja. Joe did the calculation and realized that he would have to live well into his nineties before that year's Gaja offering would be ready to drink. Thus, he made the poignant call to Signor Gaja—and then repeated the same calls to other winemakers—asking to be removed from their lists. He had enough of their wines in his cellar to last a lifetime. As a wine collector, Joe didn't have any more runway.

"Runway" is the time we've meted out to ourselves to achieve our destiny. Some of us—elite athletes, fashion models, ballet dancers, and any other "performer" relying on physical vigor or beauty, which fades with time—can calculate our runway as precisely as Joe. Many American politicians—e.g. presidents and thirty-six of fifty state governors—have term limits that detail to the day how much time they have to achieve their agenda. Most of us—artists, doctors, scientists, investors, teachers, writers, executives, and others who use our brain for a living—assume that our runway extends for as long as we retain our faculties and desire. The rest of us don't have enough information to calculate our runway or appreciate when it has ended.

There are two occasions when runway becomes a major obstacle. When we're young, we tend to overestimate our runway. Money may be scarce, but time seems infinite, dampening our sense of urgency. We put off the start of our "real life" to test more appealing or fanciful options. We've got time to take a so-called gap year. Nothing wrong with that—except when indecision or inertia extends our gap year into a "gap decade" or, worse, a "gap life."

The other extreme—when we're old—is more invidious: We foolishly believe there's not enough time to achieve our next dream. We have aged out. I see this all the time when my CEO clients are approaching "retirement age." Material success is not a concern. They are willingly moving on and passing the leadership torch to the next generation. They still want meaning and purpose in their lives, but through a catastrophic misinterpretation of the significance of their past, present, and future (see chapter 5), they let their age shut down the opportunity for a fresh start. They think no one will hire or invest in a sixty-five-year-old when so many younger candidates are available.* They're staring at a broken clock, convinced that time has stopped for them.

Adults are capable of miscalculating their personal runway at any age, from twenty-five to seventy and beyond. I know

---

*They're not entirely wrong. People tend to prefer *new* over *demonstrably good.*

thirty-year-olds who, after three years of law school and a half dozen years climbing the associate ladder at a firm, realize that practicing law is not for them. It's a commonplace for young attorneys at corporate firms in the twenty-first century. Paralyzed by the prospect of restarting their career at ground zero, the young attorneys struggle in three ways: First, they treat their early disappointment as a catastrophe rather than the blessing it actually is (after all, they're escaping a job that bores them); second, they cannot imagine a next step; and third, they don't appreciate that they have two-thirds of their adult life ahead of them. That's a lot of runway, which some people find daunting. I suggest it is a lifeline.

PARENTAL INFLUENCE. OBLIGATION. Mental block. Peer pressure. Not enough time. Inertial devotion to the status quo. These are the perennial barriers that freeze us in place and leave us yearning for a new path yet unable to take the first step on that path. But these barriers are just temporary obstructions that can be pushed aside so we can move on. They are not permanent disqualifying conditions or articles of faith that we cannot rewrite or replace.

We possess offsetting attributes that enable us to find our way. They're not a big mystery. They are latent powers such as motivation, ability, understanding, and confidence that reside within all of us, waiting to be stirred to life under the right conditions. They are the building blocks of our potential. And we need to be reminded on occasion how to deploy them for our own benefit.

EXERCISE

We Now Interrupt Our Scheduled Programming . . .

This is an exercise to help you understand your programming. Imagine that you are six. Your parents have invited their best friends for dinner. After dinner, with the adults believing that you are in bed asleep, one of the guests asks what you are really like.

Assuming they will get the unvarnished truth from your parents:

- List the adjectives your parents would use to describe the six-year-old you.
- List the adjectives you would use to describe yourself today.
- What, if anything, has changed? How did it change? Why did it change?

What did you learn from this exercise that will help you plan the rest of your life?

CHAPTER 3

THE EARNING CHECKLIST

In 1976, when I was twenty-seven, I wrote my doctoral thesis on motivation, ability, understanding, and confidence, isolating them as the four cognitive and emotional qualities that people needed in order to be successful.

- *Motivation* I defined as the force that drives us to get up each morning and pursue a specific objective and also maintain that drive in the face of setbacks and reversals.
- *Ability* was having the aptitude and skills required to achieve a goal.
- *Understanding* was knowing what to do and how to do it—and also what not to do.
- *Confidence* was the belief that you can actually accomplish what you set out to do, whether you've done it before or are attempting it for the first time.

Those four attributes are still essential success factors (and not as "Duh!" obvious as you might think). Remove any one of these virtues from your toolbox and you've dramatically increased your odds of failing. It's also important to remember that these are task-specific attributes. They are not forces that apply universally to your life. For example, there is no such thing as a motivated person, because none of us is motivated to do everything. We are selectively motivated, driven to do one thing but not another. The same is true of ability, understanding, and confidence. Each is task-specific—because none of us is able to do everything, or know everything, or be confident in every situation. This was my argument in 1976, when I was twenty-seven. But forty years in the business world as an executive coach have taught me that these four attributes don't provide a full picture. My thesis wasn't wrong; it was incomplete.

Time has taught me that you can't color success only in the bold hues of desire, talent, intellect, and self-belief. You need *support*, as well as a receptive *market* for each of your specific tasks or goals.

Mind you, there are many personal assets that improve your chances for success—e.g. creativity, discipline, resilience, empathy, humor, gratitude, education, timing, likability, and so on. But when clients young and old come to me for advice about major career decisions—whether to stay or go, whether the new job is right for them, what to do next—the following are the six must-have considerations I ask about. Without good answers for each of them, there is no next step. They're as basic as the pulse and blood pressure readings your doctor takes to begin your annual physical.

1. MOTIVATION

Motivation is the reason you try to succeed at a chosen task. It's "why" you do anything. In August 1979, Ted Kennedy challenged President Jimmy Carter in his bid for reelection. Although politicians rarely took on incumbent presidents from the same party in a primary fight, Kennedy at the time was a heavy favorite to defeat the unpopular Carter. He announced his bid in a widely seen TV interview with CBS's Roger Mudd, who started with the obvious softball question: "Why do you want to be president?" Kennedy, infamously, flubbed the answer, offering a meandering, incoherent response that didn't give people a reason to vote for him and essentially ended his campaign before it began.

Like millions of Americans who watched the interview, I remember thinking, "It's not enough that being president satisfies some personal ambition to reach the top rung of the political ladder. In telling me why you want to be president, you must also reveal the specific things you want to do in the job, whether it's building roads, or feeding hungry children, or lowering interest rates" (they were hovering around 18 percent that year). I was hearing neither *why* Kennedy wanted the job nor *how* he would do it if he moved into the White House.

Motivation may be the high-octane fuel that drives our goal achievement, but it cannot be divorced from the actual doing of the specific tasks required to achieve each of our goals. That's what makes motivation one of the more misunderstood—and therefore misused—words in the lexicon of goal achievement. Several times a week I hear people describe themselves, or someone they admire, as "motivated to succeed" or "motivated to be a good boss" (or teacher or father or partner or some other broadly defined role). Used in that context, "motivated" has no meaning—because I don't know anyone who's "motivated *not to succeed*" or "motivated to be a *bad boss*." Motivation is being confused with *desire*. They may as well be saying "I want to succeed" or "I want to be a good boss." Who doesn't?

Being motivated is not merely a supercharged emotional state induced by having a goal. It is that heightened emotional state *coupled* with a supercharged impulse to do each of the specific tasks required to achieve that goal. It is incorrect to say that you are motivated to make money or lose weight or become fluent in Mandarin, even if you feel such statements are true, unless you consistently do the big and small things required to achieve such goals.

The true test of our motivation is grounded in evidence. If we want to run a marathon in under three hours, are we motivated to do each of the necessary tasks that such an arduous physical achievement requires: wake up early in the morning six times a week to accumulate our mileage goals; reconfigure our diet so that it is in the service of maximum performance; put in the hours at the gym to build our strength and flexibility to lessen the chance of injury; and summon the common sense to take a day off when our body tells us we need to rest and recover?

Anything less and we're kidding ourself about being "motivated."

As a coach helping successful people change for the better, it's not my job to judge people's stated motivations. My job is to establish their resolve. Our lives can be filled with ambiguous motivations. Rewards such as money, fame, advancement, awards, and prestige have the power either to make us try harder or to leave us asking "Is that all there is?" Obligations to our loved ones either make us proud that we answered the call to duty or bitter about what we had to sacrifice. Overconfidence and wishful thinking either push us to exceed expectations (always a pleasant surprise) or leave us puzzled by our folly ("What was I thinking!"). Who am I to say which of these are false gods and which are legitimate?

Misunderstanding our motivation and overestimating our willingness to fulfill it may be the two defining errors you'll face as you create your own life. But you need to anticipate a few other avoidable errors as you find your true motivation.

Motivation is a strategy, not a tactic. *Motive* is the reason we act in a certain way. *Motivation* is the reason we *continue* acting that way. It's the difference between impulsively going running on a sunny afternoon to release some restless energy and running six days a week month after month because you want to get fit, or lose weight, or train for a race. In identifying your motivation, be sure to grade it on its long-term sustainability—and be realistic about your ability to sustain in the face of risk, insecurity, rejection, and difficulty. Two questions: How have you responded to adversity in the past? Why will it be different this time?

You can have more than one motivation. Joyce Carol Oates, America's prodigious woman of letters, in her essay "This I Believe," identified not one but five reasons she writes: (1) *commemoration* ("memorializing a region of the world in which I have lived"); (2) *bearing witness*, because most people cannot do so for themselves; (3) *self-expression* as a "stay" against the compromises of adulthood; (4) *propaganda (or "moralizing")* to "evoke sympathy" for her characters; and (5) a love for the *aesthetic object* that is a physical book. When one motivation is lacking, another keeps her writing. Successful people can hold two or more opposing thoughts in their mind at the same time. The same goes for your motivation.

Inertia is not motivation. I know Florida retirees who play golf practically every day. Is it their love for the game or a burning desire to lower their handicap that motivates them to spend so many hours hitting a little white ball around a very large lawn? Or is it inertia—they don't have a better idea how to spend their day? If you find that you're living the same day every day, you could ask yourself the same question: Am I living my current life because it's how I choose to find fulfillment, or because I can't imagine an alternative? An honest answer is essential, but possibly too painful to bear.

So how do we zero in on a specific motivation? Experience has taught me that there is at least one universal baseline motivation guaranteed to clarify our desire to live an earned life, and it is this: *I want to live a life that will increase fulfillment and minimize regret.*

2. ABILITY

Your ability is the level of skill you need to succeed at your chosen task. Ideally, you know what you're good at and what you're bad at, and you take on tasks beyond your abilities only because you want to stretch. Otherwise you stay within your wheelhouse of superior skills. If you have a superior skill, something that sets you apart, it should go hand in glove with motivation. Staying motivated to do something you excel at should not be a problem. And yet it is.

My friend Sanyin Siang, the co-founder and director of the Coach K Center on Leadership & Ethics at Duke University, believes that each of us has at least one skill that we take for granted and are perplexed when we discover that it's out of reach for everyone else. She calls this the "liability of expertise." Perfect pitch. Supernatural eye-hand coordination. Blazing foot speed. Repeating Kendrick Lamar lyrics word for word after one listen. Such talents are a liability, says Sanyin, because they come so easily to us. As a result, they don't feel fully earned and therefore we discount the many ways they make us special. It's like having a superpower and never using it.

This is a worrisome insight. If we can't embrace ability that comes easily to us, what's the alternative? Creating a career in areas where our abilities are less than optimal, where we're in the middle of the pack and not so special? I wouldn't recommend that either.

But we're defining "ability" too narrowly here—as if it exists between being preternaturally gifted at one extreme and possessing the bare minimum skill to do the job at the other. Emotional and psychological elements—temperament, doggedness, persuasiveness, equanimity—play an equally crucial role in establishing ability. Dealing with rejection, for example, is an essential skill for salespeople and actors, no matter how silver-tongued their sales pitch or how moving their line deliveries. Oncologists spend decades in a lab testing and waiting for a cancer treatment protocol to prove effective, with no guarantee that their efforts will ever deliver a breakthrough. Their heroic defiance of failure again and again, not their biochemistry expertise, is what defines their ability to find a cure. If you want to write novels for a living, a willingness to be alone at your desk day after day is as necessary as your facility with plot, character, and dialogue. Being comfortable with solitude draws you to your desk each morning.

My mother was an elementary school teacher from the 1950s through the 1970s in rural Kentucky. When she filled in her students' report cards, she gave them a letter grade in three categories: Achievement, Effort, and Conduct. There was also a side box for Attendance. Educators back then, it seems, knew that a student's ability was more than knowing the right answers on a test. Trying, behaving well, and showing up counted too. Not much has changed for us in adulthood. Our ability is not one isolated talent; it's a portfolio of skills and personality traits that have to match up with the life we want to lead.

3. UNDERSTANDING

Understanding is your knowledge of what to do and how to do it. In my doctoral thesis, which focused on behavior in groups, I regarded understanding in terms of role perception, viewing it through the prism of order and rank. Do people understand their role in the hierarchy? For example, as an engineer, you have the same ability as all the other engineers in your department, more or less. Like them, you are a cog in a big machine. In that situation, which is how we studied organizational behavior fifty years ago, "understanding" means knowing what particular job in the machine you're expected to do—and not deviating from your role. There's no *mis*understanding between you and your superiors about your responsibilities. You stay in your lane. The lane may be more complex and crowded for, say, an emergency room doctor or a police officer, each of whom must play many roles during a work shift. But the successful ER doctor understands the job is about alleviating pain and repairing damage. The successful police officer understands it is about keeping people safe. They stay in their lanes too.

When I started working one-on-one with executives to improve their interpersonal skills, my views changed. Roles still mattered, but so did so-called "softer" attributes, such as timing, gratitude, kindness, listening, and, most valuable of all, trusting the Golden Rule. These are the values that guide us in any situation, including the pursuit of an earned life. It required a small but painful teachable moment for me to realize this.

I was invited to speak at a dinner event for an insurance company's key managers, and I completely misread my audience. I was too jocular for a group whose company had recently suffered a serious reversal.

Afterward, the CEO told me I'd offended him and his team. The evening was a disappointment for him (and his critique was torture to hear). The error was all mine, of course, and it was an error of Understanding. I'd misunderstood my role, assuming I was there as one part teacher, one part entertainer, when in fact I was the company's guest. That was my role, and I'd basically walked into their home with mud on my shoes.

Saving the situation required soft values—in this case, focusing on the CEO's disappointment rather than my shame, and observing the present moment clearly. I needed to read the CEO standing in front of me better than I'd read the room earlier in the evening. I considered offering to speak for free the next time, but given my performance, the CEO wasn't in the mood for a next time. I considered doing nothing, hoping that time would heal this wound. But in that instant I remembered the truism that customers will forgive any problem if they can see that you care enough to correct it swiftly. That's when the Golden Rule kicked in. What would I expect if the tables were turned and I were the displeased CEO? I understood what needed to be done. Although the speaking fee was significant—as much as some people make in a year—I told the CEO, "This one's on me." When the check arrived a few days later, I returned it to him with an apologetic note. I understood that both of us needed proper closure, me more than him.

Part of Understanding is knowing the difference between good and not good enough—and accepting that in any situation, we can be one or the other.

4. CONFIDENCE

Confidence is your belief that you can succeed. You acquire confidence through an imprecise alchemy of training, repetition, steady improvement, and a string of successful results, each one feeding the other. We feel confident most often when we're facing a challenge that we've successfully overcome before, e.g. speaking in public. A less appreciated source of confidence is having a special skill that other people lack. I once asked a marathoner friend—not quite elite, but dedicated to his training and someone other amateur runners paid attention to in a race—how many miles a week he had to log in order to meet his goals. "It's not about mileage," he said. "It's about developing speed so you're confident you can outrun anyone when it matters. Speed instills the confidence. The confidence creates more speed."

I knew that confidence was essential in skill sports like golf or baseball. Sports history is filled with athletes who lose their confidence and overnight can't find the fairway or throw a curve ball over the plate. But I'd never thought that it mattered in long distance running, which struck me as an exercise in brute force endurance rather than athletic skill. But I take my friend's point. When you have speed and believe you can call on it at will, you're creating a positive feedback loop that creates more speed, and thus even more confidence.

That's the beauty of confidence. It is the product of all your other positive virtues and choices, and then it returns the favor by making you even stronger in those areas. As a general rule, if you have motivation, ability, and understanding, lacking confidence is unfortunate, almost inexcusable. You have earned the right to be confident.

5. SUPPORT

Support is the external help you need to succeed. It comes to your rescue, like the cavalry, via three sources:

Support can come from an *organization* in the form of money, equipment, even office space, anything you consider a valuable resource. Support like this is not easily acquired in organizations with limited resources. You have to earn your share of the pie.

Support can come from an *individual* in the form of direction, or coaching, or instruction, or empowerment, or confidence building. These supporters can be your teacher, mentor, boss, or simply someone in authority who takes a shine to you. The latter, in my opinion, is the single greatest piece of career luck you can have (but you have to appreciate your luck). I once asked the youngest partner at a large law firm how he got to be the head of the firm's employment practice before he was thirty-five. He said, "I left my previous firm because of a toxic boss who was actively antagonistic to me. The partner I reported to here is the opposite. He told me from day one that he had a five-year plan to retire and make me his successor. If I did what he told me to do, it was my job to lose. His support made all the difference."

Support can also be a defined *group*. The curious thing about a support group is not that we need one to reach our goals, but how reluctant we are to admit it. This denial makes sense when you consider the front-and-center contributions of motivation, ability, understanding, and confidence in our success. We develop them quietly and privately as solo actors, ignoring the impact of the outside world. It also makes sense in the context of living an earned life. "Earning" something—whether it's a raise, or respect, or our entire life—implies self-sufficiency, as if our achievements come about without anyone's assistance and are therefore more glorious and honorable.

That's delusional thinking. We all need help. Accepting that fact is an act of wisdom, not a sign of weakness. Acting on it is an essential skill. This is particularly true if you work as a sole practitioner or freelancer. In organizations—corporate, governmental, or nonprofit—your support groups are built into the infrastructure. CEOs have a board of directors, managers have their weekly meetings, and the support staff, left to their own devices, instinctively form their own small cells to support one another. Feedback, ideas, and cheerleading are always there if you want them. When recent refugees from corporate life go out on their own and say they "miss the camaraderie" in a big organization, they're really admitting that they miss the support.

Here's a not-so-dirty secret of super-successful people: The smartest, most accomplished people I know are the most avid builders of their own support group and the most reliant on their group for help (and they're not shy about admitting it). I know this because I coach some of them; being in their support group is part of my job. I see how often they go beyond the walls of their organization for counsel and comfort. I see how they use the advice and how it connects directly to their success. For them, a support group is like having a higher gear to make things happen more smoothly and quickly. If it works for them, why not let it work for you?

Your support group can include anyone, even a family member or two. A half dozen people is a manageable number; more than that and the support gets repetitive or confusing. You can even have multiple support groups for different occasions, depending on how complex and varied your life is. The cast of characters can change over time as you and the world change too. My only caveat: Never be the most admired or successful person in your group (you're seeking help, not a fan base), nor the least accomplished. Somewhere in the middle is right.

6. MARKETPLACE

I've seen this so many times within families, it's practically commonplace. A sister and brother grow up in the same household, attend the same school system, and then have completely different career goals. The sister wants to be a professional with an advanced degree, say an engineer. The brother, no less focused or ambitious but preferring a dreamier, less well-charted path, bypasses the traditional college route for the life of, say, an artisanal knife maker. The would-be engineer completes her education and enters a well-established albeit highly competitive industrial ecosystem for her skills. She glides into her career because a solid marketplace of manufacturers, high-tech companies, and design firms exists for her services. There's always demand for engineers. Not so for the knife maker. If the brother's timing is off, he may begin his career at a moment when the market for his skills is overcrowded or being disrupted by some innovation. The marketplace that should have greeted him with open arms is more unruly and vulnerable to changing consumer preferences than he imagined. It may even be vanishing in front of his eyes.

Two people from the same home who knew exactly the life they wanted to create for themselves. Two different outcomes, each depending on the marketplace for their skills.

It's romantic to think that we can pursue our most ardent dreams without regard to earning a living. The fact is, not only do the vast majority of us *need* to earn a living, if only to pay our bills and provide for our families, but through rearing or inclination, most of us can't help linking our sense of fulfillment and self-esteem to our material compensation. Unless we inherited wealth, it is only after we've accumulated enough in one career that we can afford the luxury of a new career in which money doesn't matter. Anyone who relies on a paycheck knows this.

Yet every day thousands of Americans start up a business, or go back to school, or move to another part of the country, or quit their cushy job to strike out on their own—all hoping to improve their prospects for a fulfilling life—without asking the hard-nosed question: Is there a market for my product or service if I start up the business, or get my advanced degree, or move to a new town, or no longer work at a big company? Years ago one of my best friends made this mistake. He was earning a seven-figure salary as the top strategy expert at a powerful consulting firm, but he thought he could do better striking out on his own. Several of us in his support group warned him about the obvious risk in leaving a big firm, namely, that the credibility and prestigious client list that came with his position there would immediately shrink when he changed over to running his own shop. He didn't believe us. Sadly, the marketplace rejected him. Clients he counted on to jump to him chose to stay with the big company. He never recovered.

If there is no market for what you're offering (and you don't happen to be the rare visionary who creates a new industry out of thin air), all your skill, confidence, and support will not overcome that hurdle. As Yogi Berra said, "If the fans don't want to come out to the ballpark, no one can stop them."

* * *

THESE ARE THE four internal and two external factors you have to consider and check off to gauge your chances of success at any challenging task or goal. An accomplished chef will tell you that the first crucial consideration in cooking is the concept of *mise en place:* having all the ingredients for a dish in place in the kitchen, prepared and ready to go. Then the cooking begins. Like most checklists, *mise en place* is the bluntest of organizing tools, but it is also a mindset anchoring a chef's motivation, ability, understanding, and, most of all, confidence. With everything in place, the chef is liberated to create and do what she does best: turn ordinary ingredients into something extraordinary. Consider this earning checklist as your *mise en place* before taking on any challenge that matters to you. Candidly test yourself: Am I motivated to do this? And able? Do I understand how to harness my ability to get the job done? Do my past achievements make me confident that I can do this? Do I have support? Is there a marketplace that will appreciate the effort?

Each of these six factors must be aligned, each one enhancing the other. They are not à la carte. You can't be strong on five of them and weak on the other. Each one is sufficiently broad to include the qualities that are specific to you, which makes them the ideal set of fundamental questions when you confront big change. Checking each box tells us whether we have alignment or not. Here, for example, is a recap of my checklist conversation with a friend named Marie who started up a pasta sauce business three years earlier. She had been a retired food professional whose homemade sauce was so good friends kept telling her, "You should sell this." So she did. You tell me if she has alignment:

Motivation: "I get a kick out of making a special product that customers appreciate. I'm doing this for that validation, not the money. Not yet, at least."

Ability: "My first job out of college was developing recipes for food companies. I know how to write a recipe and develop something authentically new."

Understanding: "No one is born knowing how to do a start-up. You learn it as you go. I follow the Rule of Fools: Fool me once, shame on you. Fool me twice, shame on me."

Confidence: "I've created three distinct products—we call them SKUs—for the brand. It's not foolish to expect a fourth idea and a fifth to show up. It'll happen."

Support: "We entered an accelerator contest last year and we were one of five small companies chosen to be mentored for six months by experts in the food industry, mostly for the purpose of attracting investors, which doesn't interest us yet. When I don't know something, I call my mentors."

Marketplace: "People will always need ready-made sauce to put on their pasta and pizza, to stuff their peppers, to make chili. Our niche is the high end. We don't need everyone to buy, just the right sliver of the market, and those people are finding us."

Then I asked Marie if she felt aligned. "Alignment is something I felt right away," she said, "because I was enjoying myself. Two years into it, though, when we were showing a little profit, I started wondering what was the purpose of all this work if I wasn't taking a salary yet. What was the endgame? One of the mentors told me that start-ups aim either for steady profit growth or being bought out. I decided our goal was getting someone to buy us, after which we could keep at it with more resources or move on. That gave me clarity and purpose. I felt aligned again."

Marie had all the right answers. Can you say the same about the life you're living right now?

EXERCISE

Find Your Adjacency

A successful photographer can make a midlife conversion to cinematographer or director, but she probably can't remake herself into a brain surgeon. Cinematography and directing are adjacent in ability and understanding to photography (working with cameras, people, and ideas); neurosurgery is not. That's what makes adjacency an interesting consideration when we run through the checklist for creating an earned life.

If motivation, ability, understanding, confidence, support, and marketplace, all operating in alignment, are must-have factors, then adjacency is a nice-to-have factor.

When we are frustrated with our life or career and yearn for something more gratifying, it may be emotionally soothing to imagine a life that's 180 degrees removed from our current predicament. But the odds of success favor the people who do not stray too far from their expertise, experience, and relationships. That doesn't mean we're restricted to small and incremental change in our lives. The change can be huge. But it requires adjacency—some connection, however indirect, to our track record of accomplishment.

Jim Yong Kim is the biggest brain I know. An M.D. and a Ph.D. in anthropology from Harvard, an expert in global health and infectious diseases, co-founder of Partners in Health, department chair at Harvard Medical School, director of the World Health Organization's HIV vs. AIDS division, the recipient of a MacArthur "genius grant," perennially included in annual lists of influential leaders. Which explains why, in 2009, as Dr. Jim turned fifty, Dartmouth College wanted him to be its next president. Dr. Jim and I discussed the pros and cons. At Dartmouth, he'd be dealing with faculty, donors, and a notoriously fractious student body, quite a departure from a life spent tackling public health crises. On the other hand, he'd succeeded at everything he'd ever tried. He wouldn't be away from home so much. It would be a good base for his family of two young boys. And he was familiar with academic life in the Ivy League. I urged him to take it. It would be an interesting challenge.

What I forgot to consider was adjacency. Was there enough in the job that played to his scientific expertise and would motivate him the way his previous roles did? He could handle the job, but while he loved Dartmouth and its students, he wasn't using all his talents.

Three years into his presidency, the World Bank asked him to take over its mammoth organization in Washington, D.C. We discussed the pros and cons again. At first glance, running the World Bank sounded like an even greater leap into nonadjacency than a university presidency. Jim knew very little about international finance. But the World Bank is not a financial institution like JPMorgan Chase. It is a global partnership that distributes money to developing nations to eradicate poverty. Global. Partnership. Poverty. These words defined Jim's life. In Jim's mind, poverty and public health crises weren't merely adjacent. They were one and the same. If he took the job, he could redirect the World Bank's mission to reduce poverty by waging war on specific diseases that attack the most vulnerable people. This time I didn't have to convince him to make the move. He knew it was in his wheelhouse. As a result of his seven years at the World Bank, it's estimated that programs he's been associated with have saved twenty million lives. I'd sacrifice a limb or two to have that on my résumé.

Most of the time we know when our skills are adjacent to the opportunity facing us. Adjacency is an elusive concept only when our next opportunity sounds like a stretch—an uncharted departure from who we used to be and who we'd like to become. But if the adjacency exists and we find it, the stretch soon makes perfect sense. To discover your adjacency to the life you are creating, you have to find one asset in yourself that is essential for success in your new life. For example, there was a time fifty years ago when a professional athlete or coach moving into the sports broadcast booth after retirement sounded like a stretch. Not anymore, once TV executives realized that athletes *really* knew their sport and had credibility talking to fellow athletes on camera. The adjacency was the ballplayers' savviness about their sport—their mastery of the content—not their on-air delivery, which could be learned on the job.

DO THIS: List the twenty or so people in your career with whom you communicate most frequently over, say, a three-month period. Is there one standout skill or personal quality that you share with the listed people whom you most admire? If so, is it the kind of skill that can take you far in a totally different field? That is, does who you want to become match up with who you already are? Being a creative director at an advertising agency may not seem at first like the perfect training for becoming a screenwriter, but it makes perfect sense when you appreciate the two roles' adjacency: They both require a gift for storytelling. It's the same with salesmanship. If you have the ability to sell, you have adjacency to any career that requires persuasion and making people part with their money. Once you appreciate the quality that distinguishes you from other people, you begin to see all the opportunities where that skill might come in handy. Adjacency dramatically expands your options.

CHAPTER 4

THE AGENCY OF NO CHOICE

W henever possible, I avoid making choices. Look into my closet at home and you'll find a rack of more than fifty green polo shirts. On another rack are twenty-seven identical pairs of khaki pants. On the floor are a half dozen pairs of brown leather loafers, in variable condition depending on how long I've been wearing them.*

Green polo shirt, khaki pants, and loafers—think Aeronautical Engineer Circa 1976—is my business uniform. I consciously adopted the look after *The New Yorker*'s Larissa MacFarquhar noted that that's all she saw me wear during the time she was profiling me for the magazine. Soon clients who read the piece expressed disappointment if I didn't show up in a green polo shirt and khaki pants. So I obliged them. Eventually I realized that my uniform was an act of liberation. Every time I packed my bag for a business trip, which could be three or four times a week, I didn't have to agonize about what to wear. No matter the meeting or audience, it was always green polos and khakis—one more decision I didn't have to deal with. In my small world of C-suite executives and HR

---

* Some years ago I had three Bell South executives as my houseguests. I gave them a tour of my home, including my closet. When they saw the row of identical khakis, I heard one executive say to the others, "Thank goodness, I thought he only owned one pair of pants."

professionals, it gradually became my signature, not unlike (pardon the hubris of the comparison) Tiger Woods wearing a red shirt and dark pants on Sunday in the final round of a golf tournament. But unlike Tiger, it wasn't a branding exercise for me; it was one small instance of awarding myself the freedom of no choice.

Over time, choice avoidance, at least for the small choices that don't matter to me, has become one of my highest priorities. I pretty much agree to make time for any stranger who makes the effort to reach out to meet me, telling myself, "It won't make me dumber." When I need a new assistant, I hire the first well-qualified interviewee. At a restaurant, I ask the waiter, "What would you choose?" (This has the added benefit of eliminating Buyer's Remorse. You can't regret a decision you weren't tasked with making.)

This isn't sloth or indecisiveness. It's a conscious practice of dodging any nonessential choice in order to save my brain cells for the consequential decisions that occasionally arise in a day, such as agreeing to the eighteen-month commitment of taking on a new coaching client. Some people love making choices—CEOs, film directors, and interior designers come to mind. They enjoy the power of giving a thumbs-up or -down to an acquisition, or the length of an actor's hair, or the specific shade of gray wall paint. I don't. Perhaps you don't either.

Yet extensive research shows that the process of making a choice probably represents the biggest expenditure of your mental energy each day—and it leads to depletion, which can ultimately lead to bad decisions. From the benign choice of what to have for breakfast, to the snap decision of answering or ignoring a ringing phone, to the time-consuming, often nerve-rattling process of researching, test driving, and haggling with sales managers in order to buy your next automobile, they all add up to an existence that is dominated by our choices.*

To live any life, you have to make choices. To achieve an earned life, you have to make choices with an expanded sense of scale, discipline, and sacrifice.

IN THE 1960s, at my high school in Valley Station, after every major reading assignment, our tenth grade English teacher had us write an essay on any topic we wanted. The essay just had to relate in some way to the book, play, or short story we'd just finished. She called them "freestyles." In eleventh grade, our new English teacher set a similar drill, except he chose the topics. I asked him why he didn't give us freestyles. He said, "I'm doing most of your classmates a favor. Students have complained for years that they don't have any ideas. Freedom to pick their own topic is the last thing they want."

I hadn't thought about that teacher in decades until another teacher, Alan Mulally, taught me about the Business Plan Review meetings he instituted in 2006 at the Ford Motor Company when he became CEO. The BPR, as it was known, was a rigorously structured weekly meeting held at seven o'clock every Thursday morning in the Thunderbird conference room at Ford headquarters in

---

* If I asked you to keep a log of all the choices you made in a day (starting, of course, with the decision to accept or decline this request, and then your choice of paper, pad, notebook, or digital device to record the log, and then the ink color in the pen, if in fact you chose a pen over pencil over smartphone . . . you see where I'm going with this?), how many choices would you estimate you make in a day? Hint: I'm a choice-avoiding extremist and I stopped counting for my one-day log when I hit three hundred before 4 P.M.

Dearborn, Michigan, for the sixteen top managers of the company. Attendance was mandatory, if not in person, then via teleconferencing. Surrogates were not allowed. Alan would start the meeting the same way each week. "I'm Alan Mulally. I'm the CEO of Ford Motor Company. Our mission is . . ." And then he'd go over the parent company's five-year business plan, projections, and performance, with charts grading each data point under his control with the color green (on plan), yellow (improving but not yet on plan), and red (off plan). He'd finish within five minutes. Then each manager was expected to follow Alan's format note for note: name, rank, plan, and the color-coded scores grading progress on their portfolio of projects, all in five minutes. Alan also required polite, collegial behavior in the meeting: no judgment, no criticism, no interrupting, no cynical asides. "Have fun, never at other people's expense," he'd say. The BPR was a psychological safe space.

The Ford executives initially had a hard time believing that the meeting was truly a no-cynicism, no-judgment zone. This is one reason the executives balked at assigning the color red to any of their projects: They feared their colleagues' derision.

Alan shut down the sarcasm the first week simply by calling it out on the spot. All the executives got that message. Willingness to report red—i.e., admitting a weak spot in their division—took longer. No one wanted to test Alan's promise of transparency with no reprisal. A month into Alan's tenure, when the head of North America reported the first red at a shut-down Canadian production line, Alan applauded him for his honesty and visibility, a response that wasn't lost on the room. That's the moment Alan knew he had reached his leadership team. But not all of them.

Keep in mind that except for the weekly two hours of the Thursday meeting, Alan left his team alone for much of the other 166 hours. He was there to serve, not micromanage, them, believing that the transparency and decency he demanded in the BPR would eventually penetrate the rest of Ford. This process began to reset the culture. Nevertheless, two of his senior executives told him they couldn't live with his philosophy, in effect admitting that being nice felt phony and inauthentic. He told each of them that he was sorry they felt that way, but it was their choice, not his. They knew the rules, no exceptions. He wasn't firing them. They were firing themselves.

Readers of my book *Triggers* will note that this is not the first time I've devoted paragraphs to Alan Mulally's methods. I think his BPR is a brilliant management tool, the most effective strategy I've encountered to create alignment between people's stated plans and how well they execute the plan. It is a masterstroke of account-ability that more managers should emulate. But in recent years I've come to appreciate the BPR's strictures for its psychologically incisive lessons not so much about our choices but rather about what follows, namely, how we take responsibility for those choices. This is particularly apt in the context of creating an earned life.

Alan's rules for how to behave in the BPR were a gift to the executives, not, as they initially feared, a draconian attempt to con-trol them. Alan gifted his new team with what I call the Agency of No Choice. They could either behave in a positive way or find work elsewhere—which sounds like he was offering them a binary choice, except that it wasn't because the executives could have left Ford on their own steam for other jobs before Alan ever called the first BPR. Alan wasn't the one coercing their departure. He was giving them only one choice—behave and communicate in a posi-tive way in the BPR—which is effectively no choice. It was a new show. They had to commit to it or get off the stage.

This was the "no choice" part of the Agency of No Choice. Alan fostered the "agency" part by making the BPR a *weekly* event.

It's important to understand the meaning of plan in the context of Alan Mulally's Ford Motor Company. There was no mystery about the purpose of the Business Plan Review. It was in the meeting's official name: *to review the business plan.* At Ford, "the plan" was everything, and there were many plans—the overarching plan for the parent company plus sixteen plans within the plan, one for each of the sixteen division chiefs. Everyone helped formulate these plans. No one was confused. Each plan was recapped word for word, like a mantra, at the start of each executive's five-minute presentation. And it happened every week. Everyone in the BPR knew the mission, their individual targets, what had to be done to hit these targets, and when victory could be declared.

Consider the dynamic this created in the BPR. In giving the executives only one set of options—show up at the BPR, know your plan, report on your progress, practice total transparency, be nice—Alan was securing their commitment and encouraging them to display this commitment out in the open. He was creating accountability both to the group and to themselves. Every week, all the executives had to hear their colleagues announce their progress over the previous seven days—and then compare it with their own. For competitive executives accustomed to internal and external validation, the BPR was a daunting, highly motivating environment where they could either feel self-inflicted shame or well-earned satisfaction. It wasn't a difficult choice.

Making them report their numbers every week added urgency to the process. The senior managers couldn't procrastinate or allow themselves to be distracted by anything else. They had to stick to the plan.

Alan hoped they would show progress each Thursday, that they would have turned some of their reds to yellow, some of their yellows to greens. But if they didn't, he didn't jump down their throat. In fact, he applauded their honesty. A few reds didn't make them bad people. They could do better the next Thursday. If they continued reporting reds, maybe they couldn't do it alone, so he got them help. But eventually they broke through. The executives knew that. As with the mandatory attendance at the BPR, they had no choice but to do better.

That overwhelming sense of weekly urgency, absent in other parts of our lives, gave these executives agency over their future. They knew what was expected of them and that they alone were responsible for their performance. When they reported greens that were once yellows and reds, their success felt fully earned. That is the gift of Alan's BPR. He gave his executives agency to fulfill their potential. When you have only one choice, the only acceptable response is to make that choice work.

If Alan's approach can turn around a failing industrial behemoth, saddled with competition from every corner and crippling debt and liabilities, it can be reimagined and applied to turning a less-than-fulfilling life into an earned one. We'll come back to this again in part 2. But for now, let's deal with choice.

I'VE ALWAYS THOUGHT that the luckiest people on earth, at least in terms of career, are the ones who can honestly say, "I get paid to do for a living what I would gladly do for free." Musician, video gamer, park ranger, fashion designer, food critic, professional poker player, dancer, personal shopper, member of the clergy. All of them excel at what they love and love what they excel at—and the world is willing to pay for it. Whether the payday is staggering or puny, they rarely regret the path they've chosen—because it was the only path they could see for themselves. In other words, they had no choice.

Not far behind these lucky few are the accomplished people who, when asked how they came to their current station in life, reply, "It was the only thing I was good at." I've heard this line from advertising wizards and gardeners and software designers and journalists. They're not so fortunate that they would do their jobs for free, but the ease they felt in choosing their career path is identical to what the video gamer or cleric felt. They believed they had no other choice.

Creating an earned life begins with a choice—sifting through all the ideas you harbor for your future (assuming you have ideas) and choosing to commit to one idea above all the others. Easy to say, not so easy to do. Perhaps you are a restless creative type with an excess of ideas who cannot pinpoint the single idea you want to work on. Perhaps you have the opposite problem: You lack ideas and automatically default to inertia instead.

In such a tight spot, where do you begin? How do you make up your mind about the future, the sacrifices you'll have to make, who you share it with, and where it happens? How can you be sure your eventual choice offers you the best chance for achieving fulfillment rather than suffering regret?

The conventional first step is to ask yourself a question such as *What do I want to do next?* or *What would make me happier?* To which I say, Not so fast! You're putting the cart before the horse. First, you need to run through a few preliminary steps—and each of those steps should be helping you boil down your myriad options to a single point at which you really have no choice.

Creating an earned life is first and foremost a matter of

scale—of going really big on the important things that keep you on message, small on the things that do not influence the outcome. This is the secret of living an earned life: *It is lived at the extremes.* You are maximizing what you need to do, minimizing what you deem unnecessary.

I didn't appreciate this until I was forty. Given the fulfillment I've received and the relatively few regrets I've suffered as I write this in my seventy-third year, I believe I've earned my life. I credit it to some soul-searching I did three decades ago, in 1989, when it became apparent that my random but fairly linear career path was *not* heading toward the placid working-for-the-weekend life I had imagined. Lyda and I had two young children and a hefty mortgage. For the first time in my life, I was contemplating working solo—as a corporate trainer—without the backup of an organization or partners. If I succeeded at it, I'd be traveling extensively and spending more time away from my family, which worried me. This was the risky, uncharted territory that occasioned my soul-searching.

So I conducted a cost-benefit analysis of what such a life offered and demanded. Did I have the psychological and emotional resources to sustain myself and be happy? And was I willing to maximize these resources consistently over a long period of time, fighting off other priorities and distractions? In other words, was I willing to pay the price to succeed at this new path?

This wasn't a test of my motivation, ability, understanding, or confidence. I could do the job. It was an appraisal of how much I would be sacrificing. I was establishing my priorities and confronting the trade-offs I was willing to accept. Could I find balance in what some people might regard as an insanely unbalanced life?

I listed, in alphabetical order, the six factors that I believe govern our sense of fulfillment in life:

- Achievement
- Engagement
- Happiness
- Meaning
- Purpose
- Relationships

I raced quickly through the nonworldly factors of purpose, engagement, achievement, meaning, and happiness. They were links in a familiar chain: *Purpose* meant I had a reason for what I'm doing, which ensured full *engagement*, which improved my odds of *achieving* my goal, thus adding *meaning* to my life as well as a fleeting sense of *happiness*. I didn't doubt that my new gig would deliver all of these. Maximize one and the others will follow.

What remained was *relationships*, namely, my family. My concerning issue was the effect constant travel would have on my relationship with Lyda and our children.

As I considered these questions, I realized I was not facing the typical all-or-nothing binary choice that confuses so many of us, as if I were free to choose between traveling and staying home. The facts were: (a) This was my best idea for living my own life at the time, something that aligned with my training, my interests, and my desire to help people in a meaningful way; (b) It was gratifying that people wanted to hear what I had to say and I could make a living at it; and, most important, (c) Constant travel was a nonnegotiable part of the job, no different than if I were a long haul trucker or flight attendant.

In other words, I wasn't torn between two choices. I had only one choice, which, as I've said, is really no choice. The only question I faced was one of scale. What were the dimensions of my travel obligations? How many days on the road qualified as "maximizing," and what would be the consequences of "minimizing" my presence at home? I wasn't confronting a difficult choice between corporate trainer and some unknown alternative. That ship had sailed. I was merely negotiating the terms and dimensions of a trade-off.

If an earned life is one of productive overkill—of going all in on what matters—accompanied by sacrifice and trade-offs, that was the moment I got serious about earning my life. I had no other choice.

EXERCISE

Flip the Script

The first obstacle to earning your life is deciding what that life should be. If you don't have your own ideas on the subject, you're relying on luck or the assistance and insight of others. But how can you tell when a life-changing idea has been dropped into your lap? How do you prevent inertia, or your comfort with the status quo, or a failure of imagination, or any other impediment from obscuring the chance of a lifetime that's been handed to you? How do you end up with a turning-point epiphany, not a missed opportunity? It's up to you to answer that big question.

DO THIS: Although I can't command you to be more creative or to recognize the luck that's staring you in the face, I can offer a two-step exercise to help you get there on your own:

1. **Do for yourself what you have done for others.** Can you recall the times you've given someone else a piece of life-altering advice? Maybe you set up two people on a blind date and they ended up getting happily married. Maybe you alerted a friend to a job opening that was perfect for her. Maybe you've been reminded by a grateful friend of an offhand remark you made years earlier to her that she regards as a turning point in her life. Maybe you fired an employee, convinced you were doing him a favor, and later on the employee thanked you, admitting you were right, that getting sacked was the best thing that ever happened to him. Maybe you recognized something special (rather than deficient) in another person and told them they were capable of so much more.

In each case you recognized something in others that they couldn't see for themselves. That should put to rest the issue of whether you're capable of imagining a new path. You've done it for others. Do it for yourself.

2. Begin with a basic question. "What do I want to do for the rest of my life?" "What can I do that's meaningful?" "What would make me happy?" These are not basic. They are deep, multifaceted questions that should be asked throughout your life (but don't expect an easy or quick answer). Basic questions address one factor only—because for nearly all of our major life decisions we don't require four or five strong supporting reasons. One reason will do. For example, we marry people because we love them—and that explanation alone is enough to overwhelm any other reason, for or against.*

"Do you love him?" is a basic question. So is "Who's your customer?" And "Will this work?" And "Can we afford this?" And "Where did we go wrong?" And "Are you serious?" "What are you running away from?" is basic. So is "What are you running toward?" Any question simply phrased that demands a deep, soulful examination of the facts and your abilities and intentions—i.e., that elicits the hard truth—qualifies as a basic question.

The most common question I pose when I'm advising people on their next big life move is as basic as it gets: "Where do you want to live?" It's so basic that people rarely pose it to themselves. But since we all hold an image in our mind of the ideal place for us, we answer with little hesitation. Then the real thinking begins about our future: What do we imagine doing all day in this ideal place? Can we find meaningful work there? How would the people

---

*I assert this from experience. After thirty-five years in San Diego, Lyda and I moved to Nashville for one reason alone: Our grandkids live there. The fact that Nashville turned out to be a great place to live is a bonus; a better quality of life or any other reason never factored into our decision.

we love feel about this move? If we have children or grandchildren, could we tolerate living far apart from them? The specific choice of place also speaks volumes about our ideal lifestyle. People who answer "Hawaii" or "the Swiss Alps" are not envisioning the same life as people who answer "New York" or "Berlin." You can't see a Broadway show in the Swiss Alps, and you can't hike up a mountain in Berlin. Which inspires the next basic question: "What will I do there every day?" That's the value of a basic question: It forces us to come up with very basic answers, which in turn inspire more questions that need to be answered. This is how we discover how we truly feel about our life now and what we want it to look like. Sometimes we discover that we're happy with the status quo. Other times we realize we're not satisfied at all. That's when the creativity begins.

CHAPTER 5

ASPIRATION: PRIVILEGING YOUR FUTURE OVER YOUR PRESENT

Until now, we've been discussing the earned life in the context of finding a fulfilling career, stressing how difficult it is for many of us to choose and commit to what will be our life's work. "We tremble before making our choice in life," wrote Isak Dinesen, "and having made it again tremble in fear of having chosen wrong."

For many people, however, committing to a career path does not constitute an agonizing dilemma—because living an earned life to them is not a function of what they do to earn a living. The values and skills to which they aspire have little to do with professional validation or material accumulation.

I know people whose explicit life mission is "to serve." The more they can help others, the more purpose and meaning they find in their lives. In serving others, they are literally accumulating purpose and meaning, a form of wealth more appealing to them than the conventional trophies of money, status, power, and fame.

I know others who are more devoted to perfecting themselves rather than giving to others (not that there's anything wrong with that). Constant self-improvement is their defining purpose. Every task—whether it's lowering their blood pressure or elevating their emotional intelligence—is judged against an internal standard of excellence that they approach but never reach. The closer they get, however, the more the pursuit feels earned.

I also know people whose highest aspiration is spiritual or moral enlightenment—creating a feeling of contentment about their relationship to the world, regardless of material gain or, more likely, precisely because of its absence. The fewer material holdings they rely on, the more enlightenment they have earned.

I know a lot of people, especially in midlife and beyond, who can gauge their fulfillment by surveying the scene at a large family gathering in the company of their children, grandchildren, and great-grandchildren, feeling joy and validation at how many decent, productive citizens they have guided into the world. They earn their lives by trying to be responsible patriarchs and matriarchs, a job that comes with lifetime tenure yet has to be earned every day at every age.

These are but a few of the virtues and soft values ("soft" because they cannot be measured) we hope to perfect in ourselves over time as we strive for fulfillment. They highlight a distinction that sounds obvious only after the first time you hear it: Deciding *what you do each day* is not the same as *who you want to be right now* is not the same as *who you want to become*.

I didn't appreciate this distinction until I started writing this book and reflecting on whether I ate my own cooking—that is, have I lived an earned life? If so, was the earned part shaped by what I did all day or who I wanted to be or who I wanted to become? Or was it a measure of how successfully I finally integrated these three dimensions in my life, so that I could bask in a warm sense of fulfillment and say to myself, "Mission accomplished"? Could two people with identical backgrounds and identical starts to their careers each lead earned lives despite striving for different values and virtues? Is what we want to *become* more determinative in achieving fulfillment than what we do or want to *be at any given moment*? The answer to this last question, I realized, could be found in one of my most enduring friendships.

I'm an only child, but if I had a twin brother from another mother, Frank Wagner would be that person. Frank and I started out together in grad school in 1975, had the same teachers in the same classes, graduated together with doctorates in the same field of psychology, had the same mentors in the early parts of our careers, and ended up in identical roles as executive coaches, both settling in southern California, always within a two-hour drive of each other. We've both been married for more than forty years, each with two children. We're the same age. And we have the same philosophies about helping people change their behavior. When I'm unavailable to work with would-be clients, I recommend they work with Frank. There's very little daylight between how we prepared for a career, organized our family life, and what we wanted to do professionally.

But that's where the similarities end.

In many ways, deciding who we want to become is like adopting an ideology or credo for our life, a single premise that we rely on to interpret our past and determine our present and future. Frank's guiding premise—his ideology if you will—was *balance*. He aspired to live a balanced life in which all the facets that shape a well-rounded character were given equal space and devotion. He was serious about his professional life, but never at the expense of other personal agendas: his role as an engaged husband and father; his physical fitness, his avocational pursuits of gardening and surfing. It was as if each aspect of his life—his responsibilities, his health, his extraprofessional passions—was portioned out in equal measure so he could achieve a perfect equilibrium. You could say he was an extremist about not going to extremes. The most radical example of his balanced approach is his body weight. His ideal weight is 160 pounds, and for half a century it's never fluctuated more than two pounds above or below that figure. If the scale reads 158 pounds, he eats more for a couple of days to return to 160. If it's 162, he eats less.

Compared to Frank's determined integration of all the parts of his life, I was (and still am) a hot mess of indiscipline and chaos. I loved my work. Workdays were fun. Days off left me bored. I didn't need the release valve of vacations, hobbies, and weekend rounds of golf. I figured that if work made me happy, I'd show up at home as a happy spouse and parent, which couldn't be a bad thing. The one year I intentionally reduced my time away from home from two hundred days a year to sixty-five days—because our kids were entering their teens, allegedly the most difficult years for parents, and I flattered myself that my increased presence at home would be needed—my thirteen-year-old daughter, Kelly, at year's end said, "Dad, you've overcorrected. You're spending too much time with us. It's okay to travel. We're doing fine."

Frank and I were two friends who had started our careers with identical résumés and opportunities but different game plans for finding fulfillment. Whereas Frank wanted a balanced life, I was comfortable with extreme imbalance. Neither of us judges the other for his choices. We were creating and living our own lives. Today, in our early seventies, neither of us is burdened with regret. We're convinced we've earned our lives. In the lifelong sprint to fulfillment (trust me, it's a sprint—it goes fast), we both have earned gold medals. How does this happen?

The answer lies in a trio of independent variables—Action, Ambition, and Aspiration—that govern any progress we make toward living the life we seek for ourselves.

- *Action*, in my operational definition, is **what we're doing now.** It refers to all the specific things we do during the day—from answering a question to paying a bill to making a phone call to the relative inaction of watching television for hours on a Sunday afternoon. Whether our Action is active or passive, it reflects a conscious choice. Action's time horizon is immediate, in the moment, and therefore easy to articulate: *It happened now; we just did it.* Sometimes our Action is performed in the service of our Ambition or Aspiration. Frank excelled at this. His immediate Action at any meal, for example, was determined by his weight's divergence up or down from 160 pounds. He ate less or more accordingly. And he was equally disciplined in other parts of his life. I, on the other hand, was more unregulated in my Action—unless it was somehow related to work. Only then was I Frank's equal in discipline. The truth is, Action for most of us is an aimless activity, subject to momentary whim or, worse, our stated objectives (e.g. we take a vacation from work presumably to recharge our batteries, yet we bring work with us).

- *Ambition* is **what we want to achieve.** It is our pursuit of any defined goal. It is time-bound, ending the moment we achieve the goal. It is measurable. Our Ambition is not singular; we can contain multitudes of goals simultaneously—professional, avocational, physical, spiritual, financial. It may be the greatest common denominator among successful people.

- *Aspiration* is **who we want to become.** It is our pursuit of an objective greater than any defined, time-bound goal. We aspire to serve others, or to be a better parent, or to embody more consistently a way of living or treating other people. Frank, with his expressed devotion to leading a balanced life, excelled at this from early adulthood. I was a slow learner, never identifying a grander meaning to my life until my sixth decade. Unlike Ambition, Aspiration doesn't have a clearly marked finish line. It is a continuous process with an infinite time horizon. It defies measurement. It is an expression of our higher purpose. Our aspiring may change over time but it doesn't go away, whether we articulate it or not. We stop aspiring when we stop breathing.

It is tempting to treat Ambition and Aspiration as synonyms. But to me they are not the same. Ambition is the pursuit of a specific goal with a finish line; we are X, we want to achieve Y. When we hit Y, our specific ambition ends, until we come up with our next ambitious goal. Aspiration, on the other hand, is a continuing act of self-creation and self-validation. It is not X turning into Y. It is X evolving into Y, then Y plus, then possibly Y squared.

Ambition and Aspiration are not a duopoly governing our ability to live an earned life. They cannot function properly without the third variable, Action. I call them independent variables because we can isolate them to understand their unique properties. I can keep a log of all my Action episodes in a day or week and study them to see what I do with my time, adding up the hours I'm being productive or distracted or lazy or running errands, but none of this is meaningful unless I can attach the data to a purpose shaped by my Ambition and Aspiration. Any positive, lasting self-improvement we earn in life derives from Action working in concert with Ambition and Aspiration. When these three independent variables become interdependent, serving one another, we are unstoppable. Fulfillment is in our future, regret is off the table. Unfortunately, that doesn't happen as often as we like. And it's easier to understand than to execute.

I will deal with Action and Ambition more fully in chapter 6, where they play a prominent role in determining the risks we take and the risks we run away from. But in this chapter I will focus on Aspiration—to establish how radically it differs from Ambition and why so many of us can articulate our ambitions but not our aspirations—and vice versa.

THE REASON WE find it so hard to create our own life, or even why we balk at making any kind of change, regardless of the specifics, is that we do not know in advance what our newly imagined life will feel like or whether we'll like it. That's because there's no hard stop to one phase of life that immediately jump-starts our next life phase. We do not radically alter from old us into new us in the course of a day. It's a long and gradual process enlightening us with glimpses of our future along the way. This is the process that the University of Chicago philosopher Agnes Callard calls "aspiration" (her book on the subject is fittingly titled *Aspiration: The Agency of Becoming*).

Consider the decision to have children, a big life choice and unlike all our other choices because it not only creates a new life for us as parents but literally creates the new life of our child. Before becoming parents, we are free to enjoy our childlessness, perhaps by working fourteen hours a day, or going rock climbing on weekends, or taking cooking classes at night. We know that having a child will curtail our lifestyle—and it's possible we'll resent the loss of our unencumbered time. But we do not know that for sure, nor can we anticipate the fulfillment we find in cradling our baby for hours until she falls asleep or all the other baby duties we dreaded in our pre-parental life. Aspiration is the bridge between childlessness and becoming a parent. The nine months of pregnancy, dominated by elation, anxiousness, preparation, prenatal tests, and self-care, are part of the aspiring process as we try on the emotions and values we hope to acquire one day. It's like a summer internship—when we test-drive a new job—only with an enormous lifetime commitment at the end. Professor Callard says we should not think of becoming a parent as a single discrete event when we decide to have a child. It's a process: "Old Person aspires to become New Person." There's something heroic about our aspiration, she believes, because we have an "anticipatory and indirect grasp" of the goodness to which we're aspiring. We aspire with no guarantee that we'll get what we came for or be happy with it when we do.

Aspiration, says Professor Callard, is "the rational process by which we work to care about something new." It gives us agency over our acquisition of values, skill, and knowledge. But that acquisition is not instant; it proceeds over time, demanding patience. It lets us dip our toes into the water to see if we like it before committing to a long swim, largely on our own terms, unrushed and unpressured. In that sense, the process of aspiring is like a journalist's research and reporting on the way to writing a story. The journalist does not know the full story at the start, nor does she know how it ends until she's finished investigating and interviewing, nor does she know the story's meaning until she gathers all her materials and writes it. Writing the story involves deletion, revision, midcourse corrections, frustrating stops and restarts, and sometimes abandoning the enterprise altogether. The journalist did not know any of this when she started. As the words and pages accumulate, she gets closer to fulfilling her initial intention. This aspirational act—an act of bridging Old Person with intention to New Person who is realizing that intention—is how she experiences fulfillment rather than regret.

There is another difference between ambition and aspiration that deserves our scrutiny. Ambition, when we achieve it, delivers a feeling of happiness that we cannot hold on to and protect. We get the promotion, win the club championship, or finish the marathon in under three hours. We celebrate the achievement. For a brief period, we're happy (or, more likely, not quite as happy as we thought we'd be). Then the feeling dissipates and, channeling our inner Peggy Lee, we ask, "Is that all there is?"

A friend told me this story about his school days: At age nine he was sent away by his single working mother to a K–12 school for boys who were either orphans or, in his case with one surviving parent, "semi-orphans." He lived on school property year-round with twelve hundred other boys, all expenses covered. It was the first time he had good teachers who cared about his education. He became serious about his studies. On a back wall in the school's assembly hall, the school's founder had installed an honor roll of rectangular plaques in two columns with the names of the valedictorian and salutatorian in each graduating class since 1934.

"The only ambition I had in high school," said my friend, "was to get my name on that wall as either first or second in my class. My goal was to leave a permanent mark on the school. A week before graduation, after the final exam grades were in, the school principal called a classmate and me into his office and congratulated him as valedictorian and me as salutatorian. And that was it. No medal, no framed certificate, no photo for the local paper, no speaking slot at commencement. Not even a ceremony at the wall as our plaques were put up. Our names would be enshrined on the wall at some point after graduation. By then I was living a hundred miles away with my mother, working a summer job and looking forward to college. I'd devoted my adolescence to one ambition and enjoyed the triumph for precisely the ten minutes I was in the principal's office. The funny thing is, I've never actually seen my plaque on the wall."

I guarantee that you have felt a similar emotion dozens of times since childhood. You have a goal, hit it or miss it, experience a fleeting emotion on a spectrum from elation to indifference to shame, then move on. It's as if you're hitchhiking and your ambition is the vehicle that picks you up and takes you to your immediate destination. On arrival, you step out of the vehicle, look around, and decide whether to stay in place or hail another vehicle to take you to the next destination. This is the rinse-and-repeat rhythm of an ambitious life, although—and this is important—not necessarily a happy or fulfilling life.

Aspiration, because it is all about learning "to care about something new," directs you to something more lasting than ambition, more worthy of developing and protecting. Professor Callard gives the example of aspiring to become more knowledgeable about classical music. So let's try that on.

You decide that acquiring a taste for classical music is a worthwhile project. Your reasons may be noble (it's regarded as a high art form and you're curious to learn whether its greatest practitioners—Bach, Mozart, Beethoven, Verdi—are all they're cracked up to be). Your reasons may be practical (you want to check off another status marker of being well educated). Or they may be self-serving (you want to keep pace with your more erudite friends). Or maybe you heard a famous classical piece in a movie—Pachelbel's "Canon" or Barber's "Adagio for Strings"— and yearn for more. The point is, you're curious and willing to make the effort with no idea of how it will play out. You cannot predict whether you'll be fascinated or bored, or whether this new value you've decided to acquire will actually feel valuable. So you read books, listen to recordings, go to concerts, meet a new community of friends who share your interest—and over several years build up an enviable base of knowledge that was unimaginable to you a few years earlier. This is the gift of aspiring: Even when you've moved on to another self-cultivation project—say, becoming skilled at cabinetmaking—you will always have that acquired base of knowledge about classical music, as if it's a skill or a moral value that has become part of your identity. Such a base doesn't fade away like the momentary happiness of achieving an ambitious goal. It is something you can build on for the rest of your life.

Understanding aspiration is a huge—but not wholly appreciated—difference maker in our ability to create our own life. Countless times I have heard people, especially young people, balk at taking a risky career move because they need certainty that the outcome will be positive, that the risk will pay off with a reward. They do not see that a choice that comes with a guaranteed result is, by definition, not a risk. Nor do they appreciate that aspiring to something—for example, becoming a lawyer—is an incremental process that gradually reveals its own value and, if we're lucky, continues to enhance its value for the rest of our lives.

When we aspire to be a lawyer, we go to law school, and over three years of classes and lectures and late night study, we experience detours, surprises, and hardships that deliver an outcome we could not imagine on our first day of class. We either become fully engaged with the law or conclude it's not the life for us. Only by aspiring to something—by enjoying, enduring, or despising the process—do we know which outcome we prefer. We must engage in the aspirational experience in order to understand the fulfillment it will or won't provide going forward. We cannot simply imagine it.

It's an exquisitely simple dynamic either way. Best case: In aspiring to be a lawyer, we learn to love the law. In loving the law, we become more devoted to it, thus becoming an ever better lawyer. Worst case: We find something else to devote our lives to.

This is also what makes aspiration one of the more effective regret avoidance mechanisms in our lives. Dodging regret is not the point of aspiration; it's a built-in bonus. At every point in the aspiration process, we get marginally closer to knowing whether our efforts will be satisfying or futile, which also suggests that at any point, especially if we're miserable, we can reverse course— before regret settles upon us.

For example, let's say that you hit a roadblock midway through your aspirational campaign to discover the delights of classical music. You don't feel the joy and elevated appreciation for the music that you hoped for, or you're unwilling to continue making the effort to satisfy your original intention—the listening, the concertgoing, the learning to read a musical score. A challenging aspiration has become a chore, and you have learned enough. There's nothing stopping you from putting an end to this particular aspiration long before you regret the wasted time and energy. Nor is there shame or failure in retreat. (The best field generals are masters of retreat as well as attack.) Unlike your ambitions, which are not easily concealed from others, your aspirations are private matters, involving your pursuit of hidden capabilities and values. You alone know what you're up to. You alone judge the outcome. You alone perceive the slow but steady creation of a new you. You alone earn the sense of fulfillment that comes with working to care about something new. And you alone have the power to call it off.

I appreciate the irony that while I'm extolling aspiration as an essential motivating function that lifts us to perfect our noblest instincts, I'm also saying that it has a valuable braking function, like an early warning system telling us to stop and rethink what we're doing. Don't let this double role confuse you. Aspiration is your best friend, whether it motivates you or tells you to stop wasting your time. It's certainly an improvement on achieving a long-held ambition only to end up asking yourself, "Is that all there is?"

* * *

MY CLIENTS AND other coaches "get it" when I explain the
Action/Ambition/Aspiration model to them. Their initial takeaway is that the Triple A's (as I fondly call them) are three independent variables and they are not necessarily connected.
We have to make them so. They get the fact that Action for too
many people is random and unfocused, serving no other purpose than satisfying impulse or immediate need. People cook
dinner because they're hungry. People go to work because they
need a paycheck. People watch their favorite teams play at the
neighborhood bar because that's what their friends are doing.
These are justifiable actions, not necessarily grim and joyless,
but what goal achievement or even higher purpose are they connected to?

Then I put this chart in front of the clients and coaches.

Activity	ACTION	AMBITION	ASPIRATION
Time horizon	Immediate	Time-bound	Infinite
Profile	What you do	What you want to achieve	What you want to become
Definition (Write as much as you like)	....	....	....
	....	....	....
	....	....	....
	....	....	....
	....	....	....
	....	....	....
	....	....	....

I go around the room asking them to fill in the blanks. I'm curious to see how many of them have successfully integrated a specific Action to a defined Ambition to the Aspiration in their lives. The successful executives and leaders have an easy time defining Action and Ambition but often draw a complete blank on Aspiration, as if they've never considered it. I'm not surprised.

The vast majority of the successful business people I know live a life dominated by Ambition. Because they are highly motivated to achieve specific goals, they have the discipline to subordinate their Action to their Ambition. The two are in sync.* If they're not careful, however, especially in a competitive business environment where hitting targets is how we keep score, their discipline can easily turn into goal obsession. Like politicians who campaign on Aspiration (their higher ideals) but, because politics is messy and compromising, govern on Ambition (their need to win the next election), the executives are at risk of forgetting their values and their original reason for planting the goal—namely, to serve their Aspiration. In the same way that the arena of hardball politics can corrupt politicians, the environment the executives work in can corrupt them. An all-too-common example: Because of their goal obsession, the executives neglect the people they claim they're

* I don't know many executives who would not include being recognized as a superior leader near the top of their Ambition list. One of the things I teach them to do is suppress some of their harsher judgments and comments in the workplace—because superior leaders don't create a toxic environment. They strive to be universally kind and generous, even among disappointing colleagues who may deserve tougher love. Should they have lapses, forgetting that their daily interpersonal behavior is supposed to be serving a major career goal, that's when I'm called back in—to remind them of their Ambition and help them realign their Action with it.

working for, namely, the people they love. They have become lost in their Ambition, regardless of whether they've defined their Aspiration or articulated their higher values. They might as well be hitting targets in target practice.

Responding to the chart, many of the coaches, who tend to be a well-meaning, idealistic bunch, fill in the blanks differently. They're quite clear on Aspiration—e.g. being present, serving others, making the world a better place—but fuzzy about the actions and goals they're pursuing to serve their aspiration. They're reluctant to do the hard, uncomfortable things required in this online era—mostly the performative "hand shaking" with the marketplace via social media, writing, and public speaking—to expand their reach and help more people. True, they're making a living and doing good, but they're falling short on Aspiration because they haven't adequately linked it to Action and Ambition. In many cases, they have never clarified what their Action and Ambition should be.*

IN THIS SHORT course in Aspiration Appreciation, I've saved the best point for last, because it dovetails so nicely with the point I made in chapter 1. In that chapter, I urged you to consider the Every Breath Paradigm as a Buddha-inspired new way of understanding your self and your place in the continuum of your time

---

* At this moment in August 2021, here's how I'd fill in the blanks. My Aspiration is to "create a maximum benefit for as many people as I can in the time I have left to do it." My time-bound Ambition is to "publish a book called *The Earned Life* in 2022." My Action is to "stay at my desk and write all day." In this instance I have alignment. What I'm doing at present is consistent with my goal for next year, which in turn serves my more distant dream of helping as many people as possible.

on earth. Your self is a countless series of selves comprising old self and current self and future self, changing from one to the next with every breath you take. Among its many virtues, Aspiration is also the mechanism that best supports and clarifies this paradigm. (That "aspiration" stems from the Latin *aspirare*, meaning "to breathe," is a delightful illumination.)

Remember twenty-one-year-old Curtis Martin, who, despite his reservations, decided to play in the NFL as an investment in his future self? He didn't play for the love of the game. He didn't know whether he'd succeed in the NFL, where the average length of a running back's career is three years. He risked concussions, brain damage, permanent physical debility—which is like going off to war, although no one thanks you for your service. But it was an acceptable risk. In aspiring to a post-NFL self, he was creating separation from all his previous selves and, through the acquisition of new values and self-knowledge during his eleven-year Hall of Fame career, becoming a totally unexpected person.

At its core, Aspiration is an act of privileging your future over your present. Think of it as a transfer of power from old to new. No matter how risk-averse you think you are, when you aspire, you are choosing to be a little bit of a gambler. Using the currency of your time and energy, you are betting that the future you will be an improvement on the current you. Don't be surprised how tenaciously and creatively you try to win that wager. It is how a life is earned.

EXERCISE

The Hero Question

We all need heroes. It is a need so strong that every narrative we encounter—whether it's a short story or a film or a joke—must contain a clear hero figure in order to hold our attention. When we can't locate the hero (or antihero), our interest collapses. Heroes exist to receive our admiration and provide us with inspiration. This is not a controversial notion. But I required my friend the Turkish-born industrial designer Ayse Birsel to help me take our fascination with the heroic one step further—beyond admiration and inspiration all the way to aspiration.

It began with a simple question after I had spent hours prodding participants in one of Ayse's Design the Life You Love seminars to be bolder in deciding what they wanted to do next. At some point, one of them turned the tables on me:

"If you think it's so easy, what's next for you?" one of them said.

I went blank. Ayse, a master problem solver, tried to help.

"Let's start with a simple question," she said. "Who are your heroes?"

That was easy. "Alan Mulally, Frances Hesselbein, Jim Kim, Paul Hersey, Peter Drucker. And, of course, Buddha," I said.

"Why?" she asked.

"Well, I'm a Buddhist. And Drucker, who became a mentor late in his life, was the greatest management thinker of the twentieth century."

"Okay, but what's 'heroic' about them other than you like their ideas?"

"They gave away everything they know to as many people as

they could, so others could pay it forward. Even though Buddha's been dead twenty-six hundred years and Peter died at age ninety-five in 2005, their ideas survive," I said.

"Why not be more like your heroes?" she said.

That was the moment I realized I could do more than admire my hero-teachers. I could adopt their ideas. I could aspire, however modestly, to become what most impressed me about them. Thus began my aspiration to share what I know, the execution of which did not jell right away in my mind. But Ayse had planted the seed, and it grew, which is how—long after I had concluded that I didn't have one more "next big thing" in my life, that my aspiring days were behind me—I "accidentally" formed my small community of like-minded people known as 100 Coaches (which I'll explain in chapter 10). If I can do it, you can too.

DO THIS: We place our heroes on pedestals too high to reach, rarely considering them as role models to copy. The four steps in this exercise correct that error:

- Write down the names of your heroes.
- Write down one-word descriptors of the values and virtues that endear them to you.
- Cross out their names.
- Write your name in their place.

Then wait for your next big aspiration to appear.

EXERCISE

Resolve Your Dichotomies

This exercise is also inspired by Ayse Birsel (and it also involves crossing out words, so keep your Sharpie handy). In 2015, when she was launching her Design the Life You Love seminars, she asked me to bring a few friends to one of her first outings in New York—to fill up seats, since only six people had signed up. I brought seventy. If Ayse was nervous or intimidated by the big crowd, I couldn't detect it. But I also knew that talking for an hour or more to an audience of several dozen strangers requires a little more projection of personality than talking to six people. Six people is a dinner party, six dozen is an audience. So I decided to help raise her energy level.

Ayse had once told me, "If I were stranded on an island and could only have one creative tool, it would be dichotomy resolution." Her favorite part of product design was resolving either/or decisions the client left to her discretion, e.g. whether the design should be classic or modern, small or functional, a stand-alone or expandable into a product line, and other choices. Ideally, in design, it's a mash-up of both—a classic design but updated with modern materials, such as the Ford F-150 pickup with an aluminum body instead of traditional steel. But the dichotomies in our everyday behavior seem to demand resolution rather than forced integration. Optimist or pessimist? Joiner or loner? Active or passive? Pick one or the other; you can't be both.

Remembering her affinity for dichotomies, I took Ayse aside moments before the seminar began.

"I don't know if you've ever resolved the extrovert versus introvert dichotomy in your life," I said, "but today's not the day to choose introvert. Let's sing." I started singing "There's No Business Like Show Business." Amazingly, she knew the words and joined me. Afterward, when she finished laughing, I told her, "Remember this feeling. The audience isn't here for another business meeting. This is showtime."

Half of us see the world in black and white; the other half see shades of gray. Like Ayse, I'm in the first group (the previous sentence is proof). If you're like me, you know that seeing the world as an endless string of dichotomies won't automatically simplify your decision making. You've merely reduced your many options to two. You still have to choose one. This is especially critical at the start of the aspiration process. Unless you're hoping to flip your personality completely, your aspirations should not be in stark conflict with your core preferences, virtues, and quirks. You need to identify the dichotomies that regularly reappear in your life, especially when they're a recurring source of problems or failure (e.g. procrastination as opposed to timeliness). Then you have to resolve them, deciding which half you want to own.

DO THIS: Step one, list as many interesting dichotomies as you can think of. (I've provided forty to get you started; feel free to add your own.)

Step two, use a Sharpie to redact completely each unchecked dichotomy that doesn't really apply to you.

Step three, study the remaining dichotomies to determine which half of each pairing reflects you. Are you a leader or follower? Life of the party or wallflower? Present or distracted? Ask partners or friends for their opinion if it helps. Now, cross out the half of the pairing that doesn't apply. You should end up with a sheet of blacked-out words that looks like a government redaction of a CIA agent's memoir.

STEP 1 Make a list		STEP 2 Cross out things that don't matter to you		STEP 3 Cross out one of the two remaining pairs	
Glass Half Empty	Glass Half Full	Glass Half Empty	Glass Half Full	Glass Half Empty	Glass Half Full
Let It Go	Hold On To It	Let It Go	Hold On To It	Let It Go	Hold On To It
Talent	Hard Work	Talent	Hard Work		
Judgmental	Accepting	Judgmental	Accepting	Judgmental	Accepting
Famous	Anonymous	Famous	Anonymous	Famous	Anonymous
Patience	Impatience	Patience	Impatience		
Conservative	Progressive	Conservative	Progressive		
Indoor	Outdoor	Indoor	Outdoor		
Town	Country	Town	Country		
Serious	Fun	Serious	Fun	Serious	Fun
Leader	Follower	Leader	Follower	Leader	Follower
Giver	Taker	Giver	Taker	Giver	Taker
Insider	Outsider	Insider	Outsider		
Reason	Feeling	Reason	Feeling		
Trusting	Suspicious	Trusting	Suspicious	Trusting	Suspicious
Thoughtful	Impetuous	Thoughtful	Impetuous		
Risk-Averse	Risk-Friendly	Risk-Averse	Risk-Friendly	Risk-Averse	Risk-Friendly
Money Matters	Money Doesn't Matter	Money Matters	Money Doesn't Matter		
Lack of Time	Lack of Money	Lack of Time	Lack of Money	Lack of Time	Lack of Money
Balanced	Unbalanced	Balanced	Unbalanced	Balanced	Unbalanced
Quiet	Loud	Quiet	Loud		
Need To Be liked	Don't Need To Be liked	Need To Be liked	Don't Need To Be liked	Need To Be liked	Don't Need To Be liked
Short Term	Long Term	Short Term	Long Term	Short Term	Long Term
Accept Your Culture	Reject It	Accept Your Culture	Reject It		
Decisive	Indecisive	Decisive	Indecisive	Decisive	Indecisive
Showboat	Wallflower	Showboat	Wallflower	Showboat	Wallflower
Ironic	Sincere	Ironic	Sincere		
Proactive	Reactive	Proactive	Reactive	Proactive	Reactive
Status Quo	Progress	Status Quo	Progress	Status Quo	Progress
Deep	Shallow	Deep	Shallow	Deep	Shallow
Employed	Self-Employed	Employed	Self-Employed	Employed	Self-Employed
Married	Single	Married	Single	Married	Single
Travel	Work at Home	Travel	Work at Home	Travel	Work at Home
Internal Validation	External Validation	Internal Validation	External Validation	Internal Validation	External Validation
It's Not Fair	I'm at Peace with It	It's Not Fair	I'm at Peace with It	It's Not Fair	I'm at Peace with It
Procrastinate	On Time	Procrastinate	On Time		
Confront	Avoid	Confront	Avoid	Confront	Avoid
Pragmatist	Dreamer	Pragmatist	Dreamer		
Present	Distracted	Present	Distracted		
Delayed Gratification	Instant Gratification	Delayed Gratification	Instant Gratification	Delayed Gratification	Instant Gratification

The remaining unobscured words when you're done reveal your defining qualities. You can't argue with the picture they paint. You painted it. These qualities influence not only what you aspire to but whether or not you will earn it. Bonus round: Share (if you dare) your finished sheet with the people who know you best. For valuable feedback.

CHAPTER 6

OPPORTUNITY OR RISK: WHAT ARE YOU OVER-WEIGHTING FOR?

Remember Richard, the young taxi driver we met on page one of the Introduction who made a colossal error that he's regretted all of his adult life? When Richard told me his sad story of not showing up for an arranged first date with a wonderful young woman he'd met a week earlier while driving her from the airport to her parents' home, I thought his choice was inexplicable. But as I've thought about it over the years and discussed it with Richard, I believe I understand why he froze three blocks from his date's door and turned around, never to see her again. Richard's error was not the result of a sudden bout of stage fright or cowardice; those were the effects but not the cause of his poor decision. His mistake was a failure to properly weight the opportunity and risk that the first date was presenting to him. He over-weighted the risk, under-weighted the opportunity. And thus he missed the opportunity.

In this unfortunate miscalculation he was not alone. Each of us does it all the time.

We'll get back to Richard's error in a moment, but first let's probe a little more deeply into the relationship between opportunity and risk—and why we so often fail to balance the two, leading to poor choices.

*   *   *

OPPORTUNITY AND RISK are the two key variables you should be considering in any "investment" decision, whether you're investing material resources or your time, energy, or allegiances. Opportunity represents the magnitude and probability of *benefit* derived from your choice. Risk is the magnitude and probability of *cost* incurred by your choice.

When our choices are heavily weighted in favor of either side of the opportunity-risk decision* —and you can gauge that balance accurately, if not perfectly—it's easy to make a decision that will let us sleep at night. If we believe that our choice will almost certainly produce a big benefit with virtually no chance for loss, we will make it. If we believe that our choice will almost certainly provide huge loss with no chance of gain, we will avoid it.

Sometimes we're worried about the risk. So we seek information that helps us balance the risk with the attractive opportunity. For example, you want to go on vacation in a warm, sunny climate not too many time zones away from your home in Boston. You choose a Caribbean island that fits the bill. The major risk is when to go. You don't want to take your vacation when the weather is

---

*This type of decision is more commonly referred to as a risk-reward decision. That's a misleading term, in my opinion, because it improperly joins risk and reward at the hip. Do one, get the other. It presumes that if we take the risk, the reward is inevitable. That's nonsense, of course. Where's the risk if the reward is inevitable? I prefer "opportunity" because it more accurately describes what's at stake. The benefit of taking a risk is not the reward itself, but rather getting the opportunity to earn the reward. A risk is not foolish simply because we didn't realize the anticipated reward. Other factors, far beyond our control, can negatively affect the outcome. When we take a risk, all we're doing is choosing to seize an opportunity. The reward may or may not come later.

unreliable. So you google weather patterns in the island of your choice and learn that June through August are too hot, September is hurricane season, October and November are too wet, and December and January offer the fewest hours of daylight. March and April, you conclude, are the perfect months to take a break from the bitter New England winters—lots of sunshine and daylight hours, minimal chance of rain. This is how you balance risk and opportunity and make a choice that improves the probability of having a great vacation. There's no guarantee, but you're close enough for comfort. Thank you, Google.

Sometimes the opportunity overwhelms the risk, and your only risk is failing to accept that a unicorn—the mythical too-good-to-be-true opportunity—has walked into your life. Let's say you have the opportunity to buy one hundred widgets at the distress sale price of $1 a widget. Because you follow the market for widgets very closely, you alone happen to know someone who desperately needs those one hundred widgets and is willing to pay as much as $10 a widget for them. Unlike you, this customer doesn't know that they can be had for $1 a widget. The customer's ignorance in this instance is your edge. You buy the widgets for $100, sell them for $1,000, and pocket the difference— a 900 percent return on your investment. Absent the highly unlikely event that the widget market collapses in the brief interval between acquiring and unloading the widgets, this is as close to an all-opportunity, no-risk decision as you can make. This sort of thing happens thousands of times a day in bond markets and commodity exchanges. Someone believes pork bellies are underpriced, buys them cheaply, and sells them for a profit to someone else who urgently needs them (or believes you're still underpricing them). It's the sort of complex calculation, involving millions of dollars, that benefits from the backup of sophisticated software and high-speed supercomputers.

You'll notice that in each of these choices where money is changing hands—and financial risk is incurred—there is a system and infrastructure, in the form of powerful technology rapidly delivering historical data for calculating the balance between opportunity and risk, that improves your ability to make a defensible choice—and, I might add, reduces your chances of making a foolish one. A lot of business decisions are made with that data-driven advantage; it's better than overrelying on emotion or intuition.

Not so in everyday life. There are few useful metrics to help us balance opportunity and risk when we're choosing, say, whom we should marry, or where we should live, or the right time to switch careers. These are some of the biggest life decisions we make, overloaded with consequence and the potential for regret, and we don't have many instructive tools to ensure that we choose wisely. Instead, we choose hastily and impulsively. We're influenced by our memory of past successes and blunders, or by the opinions of others. Worst of all, we let someone else make the choice.

What if there was a method or conceptual structure that reduced the emotion and irrationality that governs our risk choices and helped us become better choosers?

Honoring the trial attorney dictum of never posing a question for which one doesn't know the answer, I have an answer.

It's found in the same trio of independent variables—the Triple A's of Action, Ambition, and Aspiration—that we introduced in chapter 5. The distinguishing characteristic of each variable for me is its time horizon. How far out from the present moment is each variable pointing? Is it minutes, years, or a lifetime?

Aspiration refers to all the things we do in the service of a higher purpose in our life. Its time horizon is infinite. There's no finish line to our aspiring.

Ambition represents our focus on achieving defined goals. It operates in a time-bound dimension, determined by how long it takes to achieve a goal. Ambition can race or crawl toward a finish line, depending on the complexity and difficulty of the goal. We can resolve ambition in days or months or years—and then move on to the next goal.

Action represents our activities at a specific moment in time. Action's time horizon is immediate, forever in the now. It doesn't serve any purpose other than our immediate need. We wake up hungry, so we eat breakfast. The phone rings, so we answer it. The light changes from red to green, so we step on the accelerator. Most of the things we do under the Action umbrella are reactive, not particularly well considered or even within our control. Our Action is often attached to puppet strings—and we're not necessarily pulling the strings.

Distinguishing these three time dimensions and seeing how well they serve one another (or not), I believe, can have a marked influence on how close we come to living an earned life. As I've noted, many of the CEOs I work with face the temptation of residing almost entirely in the Ambition dimension. They are always aiming at targets and using (or suborning) their Action to serve their Ambition. Aspiration in the form of seeking and serving a higher purpose in their lives hardly ever enters the picture, at least not until they near the end of their CEO life and wonder, "What was all this for?" It seems to be the opposite for my more high-minded and idealistic colleagues and friends. They over-weight Aspiration at the expense of Ambition. They dream big and do small.

What I want you, the reader, to see is that our lives can be more fulfilling when we align these three variables so that Action is synced with Ambition is synced with Aspiration.

The additional point I want to make now is this: The dynamic of aligning Action to Ambition to Aspiration also applies to our risk decisions. The Triple A's offer a conceptual structure that helps us make better choices. Facing the choice of accepting a serious risk or rejecting it, we need to pause to ask ourselves which time horizon the risky choice is serving: Is it our long-term Aspiration or our shorter-term Ambition, or does it fall into the Action category, serving little more than the short-term stimulation that comes from filling an immediate need? If we know that, we know when taking a risk is worth it and when it is not. And presumably we will take smarter risks that turn our opportunities into fully realized rewards.

For example, when I was twenty-seven and living in Los Angeles, I loved going to Manhattan Beach in a wet suit with my boogie board. I wasn't an experienced surfer riding a big board standing up. I was a novice riding a boogie board on my belly. But the sun, the surf, and the small frisson of danger when I caught a wave, however small, were thrilling and addictive. On one particular day, I was out with my friends, Hank and Harry, and feeling particularly bold. You have two choices out on the water: small wave or bigger wave. You get more rides with the small waves, but the excitement is small compared with the big waves that the veteran surfers waited for farther from shore. As the day wore on, the waves got bigger. With each successful ride of a small wave, Hank, Harry, and I egged on one another to try a big wave.

I could feel my confidence and adrenaline level rising under the mutual goading. I timidly inched farther and farther out to where the better surfers were waiting for the big one. On the horizon, I could see a large swell approaching. I paddled toward the nine-foot wave, which from my prone position on the boogie board looked like a mountain about to engulf me. Not surprisingly, my timing was off and I was swallowed up by the wave and driven with great force headfirst into the shallow ocean floor. My neck was broken in two places, C5 and C6. For a while I was not sure that I would walk again. I lost the use of my left arm for nine months. But I eventually recovered. Three less fortunate surfers that summer with similar injuries never walked again.

During the two weeks I was lying on my back in the hospital, I had lots of time to savor the mixed emotion of regretting my decision while feeling grateful that I wasn't paralyzed or dead. If I had appreciated the Action-Ambition-Aspiration triad back then, I might or might not have made a more prudent choice. But at least it would have been a fully considered choice that I would have been comfortable with, regardless of the outcome. I would have known that my aspiration in life had nothing to do with surfing. I was never going to be a great surfer. It was not an important part of who I wanted to become as a human being. I would have known that my ambition for surfing was strictly confined to developing enough proficiency to enjoy myself without risking injury. I also would have seen that my actual choice was guided by Action, all in the service of an immediate thrill that was not in sync with who I was or wanted to become. But I'd like to think that if I'd had the Triple A's back then as my risk decision tool, I would have chosen differently, although I can't say for sure. (Using the Triple A's lessens our irrationality, it doesn't cure it.) Today I know I would have.

OUR MISTAKES IN calculating risk and opportunity don't have to be dramatic and consequential, like my broken neck. They can be small and insidious, providing immediate short-term benefit but nothing else. Consider the example of people at a casino who choose to play the slot machines. Slot machines, often called "the crack cocaine of gambling," can account for 75 percent of a casino's revenue. When we studied addiction in graduate school, slot machine addiction was the one that puzzled me the most. And it continued to puzzle me for many years. Why would people invest their money in a game that overwhelmingly favored the house over the gamblers? And everyone knew it! Although the odds vary among different machines, they are printed on each machine. And they are invariably the second- or third-worst way of winning big money in a casino.

My undergraduate degree was in mathematical economics, so I understood the equations that probability theorists used to explain the folly of playing the slots as a moneymaking scheme. Being rational human beings, the theorists were treating the slots as a financial play with a poor return on investment. I thought the same way. Being more of a rational, future-focused thinker, my problem was assuming that the gamblers' time horizon toward rewards was the same as my own. In terms of Aspiration, I could not imagine anyone finding meaning in life by spending countless hours watching flashing lights on a video display. In terms of Ambition, I could not imagine anyone setting a goal to become a world-class slot machine player. Eventually I came to see that Aspiration and Ambition had nothing to do with playing the slots. The people stationed like statues at the slot machines for hours weren't there to achieve a long-term benefit. That was too far off in a hazy future to interest them. Their time horizon was strictly in the Action dimension, focused on the next pull of the lever, then the next one, and the next, until they got bored or ran out of money (on average, a player starting with $100 will run out of money in less than forty minutes).

I began to see why so many casino patrons become slot machine addicts—they're stuck in the Action dimension—and how we all can fall into this same trap in our journeys through life. It is a matter of time horizon. With Aspiration, we are focused on the timeless, ultimate benefit of what we are doing. With Ambition, we are focused on the time-bound future benefit of what we are doing. With Action, we are focused on the immediate benefit of what we are doing. The slot players were all in on Action and its immediate benefits.

From my perspective, they were throwing money down the drain for the brief and tiny thrill of waiting to see if they "won." But given the slot players' immediate time horizon, it almost made sense. For the low cost of a dollar a pull, they accepted a low probability of a big payoff but enjoyed a high probability of experiencing immediate stimulation. The slot players were playing a game that I had failed to see—in which nearly all the benefit was as immediate as the next pull. And it was a risk they were glad to take—the payoff in short-term thrills and "entertainment" offset their losses in cash. From an investment point of view, it may have been the wisest investment they could make.

It's not a bet I'd make, though. There's nothing about playing the slots that aligns with Ambition and Aspiration in my life. It's all risk and no opportunity.

THE RISKS WE take in life should be the most informed decisions we make—because so much is at stake and the consequences can be life-changing. Using the Triple A's to review our best and worst risk decisions, as I should have done with my surfing accident, is as easy as checking off a very short shopping list. Here's how the Triple A's would have helped me on that sunny day with Hank and Harry on the water:

- Does the risk I'm taking represent an Action that aligns with my immediate need? *Yes.*
- If so, does my Action align with my Ambition? *No.*
- Does the risk align with my Aspiration? *No.*

When the noes outnumber the yeses, it's time to rethink the risk you're about to take. (In my case, I would have concluded that my only immediate need for taking on the big wave was to impress my buddies, Hank and Harry. Hardly the most persuasive reason if I had been thinking beyond the moment.) At the very least, you'll be surprised at how often you fall back on raw emotion and thoughtless impulse to take a risk.

The bigger takeaway from this split-second Triple A's checklist is obvious in hindsight: When we overfocus on Action at the expense of our Aspiration and Ambition, we tend to make very poor opportunity-versus-risk decisions. This is the classic conflict—our anticipation of a short-term benefit is engaged in a tug-of-war with our long-term welfare, and short-term is winning! And it leads to foolish risks. (Perhaps this classic conflict has cost you dearly too.)

Our other classic risk assessment error is the flip side of the same coin. It appears when our fear of the short-term cost (the risk) impedes us from seizing the opportunity to achieve a long-term gain.

This is where Richard went wrong. I've discussed it with him since he first shared the story (the young woman's name was Cathy), and we agree that the raw in-the-moment emotion governing his

regrettable choice was a potent cocktail of fears, each one a variation on the fear of being judged and found wanting:

- Fear of looking stupid (he drove a cab; she had an Ivy League
  pedigree);
- Fear of being found out (she lived in a big house in a wealthy
  neighborhood, she was out of his league);
- Fear of rejection (her parents would disapprove);
- Fear of failure (the first date would be their last date).

Richard was drastically over-weighting the risk of going on a
date with Cathy and, blinded by his fears, severely under-weighting
the opportunity at hand. If only he could have looked past his in-
the-moment fears and focused on the future—that is, if only he
could have weighed the Action he was about to take against his
reasonable Ambition of building on the relationship with Cathy
that they had started during the cab ride—not to mention his Aspiration to find a loving partner for life—he might not still be regretting his choice five decades later.

In the moments three blocks from Cathy's house, before he
turned around and abandoned her, he could have weighed Action
against Ambition and Aspiration, then reflected on his long-term
best interest. "What's the worst that can happen?" he could ask.
"Her parents don't like me. I say something stupid. We have a bad
date and I never see her again. *C'est la vie.*" And get on with his life.
He certainly would have reduced his ongoing tab of regret.

When you start experiencing fear in pursuing any opportunity,
ask yourself why. What are you afraid of, exactly? If it's the possibility that you'll experience a short-term setback, such as being
rejected or looking stupid, change your time horizon. Try to view

the experience as if you were years older. Will your rejection scar you for life, or just produce the momentary discomfort of a nick of the skin that heals quickly? Then consider the opportunity from the same vantage point. What's the best-case scenario if you seize the opportunity? What does your resulting life look like? And how do you feel about it?

THE TRIPLE A'S checklist is a simple tool that improves our opportunity to get risk right. But don't let its simplicity lure you into underestimating its importance in resolving seemingly insignificant decisions. After all, when we're making decisions that affect our ambitions and aspirations, we are dealing with some of our most major issues. The truth is, we are not very good at sifting the insignificant choices in our lives from the significant. In the moment of decision, we grossly overestimate the impact of some choices that end up being meaningless and grossly underestimate others that turn out to be life-altering. I casually decided to paddle farther from shore to catch a bigger wave and nearly destroyed my life. Richard decided to skip out on a date when he was twenty-one and is still haunted by his folly nearly fifty years later. In the same way that we are very bad at predicting what will make us happy, we are also bad at foreseeing the consequences of what we assume are minor decisions. When Ambition and Aspiration are in the mix, there are no minor decisions. Employing the Triple A's checklist won't make us perfect decision makers, but it will eliminate some of the surprise we feel when the seemingly inconsequential decisions turn out be very consequential.

CHAPTER 7

SLICING THE LOAF TO FIND YOUR ONE-TRICK GENIUS

Perhaps you noticed one glaring omission from my list of dichotomies in chapter 5. The omission is intentional. I'm referring to one of the perennial choices we face in adulthood: *Is it better to be a generalist or a specialist?*

There's no correct answer to this question. People can achieve an earned life on either path. Where you land in the generalist versus specialist debate is simply a personal preference, dictated over time by your experience. But at some point, you have to resolve this dichotomy, making a commitment to one or the other. The alternative—a loosey-goosey in-between life in which you're neither good at many things nor great at one thing—is not pretty.

Although I would never judge your choice, I'm not an unbiased observer. In fact, I'll warn you up front that I'll be resolving this dichotomy in favor of being a specialist—because that is the path I followed in my career and now I can't see any other alternative. As I say, on this issue I'm biased—and unapologetic. You've been warned.

The bare bones of my career would not predict I'd up end this way. I became a specialist without meaning to at first. After all, I have a Ph.D. in behavioral science. What's more generalized than the entirety of human behavior? But everything I've done since graduate school has been an exercise in slicing the loaf of my professional interests into ever thinner slivers of specialization.

For one thing, my interest wasn't in the broad swath of human behavior; it was in organizational behavior, i.e., a much narrower focus on how we behave during our hours in the workplace (the other hours being someone else's concern).

Next, I discovered I didn't want to work with disengaged and troubled people frustrated by their lack of success. I wanted to work with successful people. And not all successful people, just the *extremely* successful, as in CEOs and other top-tier leaders.

Continuing to slice thinner, I also told would-be clients that if they were looking for help on traditional management issues like strategy, sales, operations, logistics, compensation, and shareholders, I was not their guy. I focused on one thing: the client's interpersonal behavior. If he or she was doing something that was counterproductive among colleagues at work, I could help him or her change for the better.

This process didn't happen overnight. It took years of sampling and stumbling, of absorbing client feedback, of culling my weak spots from my portfolio and keeping what worked. By my late forties, I had sliced the loaf thin enough. I was not only a specialist in interpersonal behavior in the workplace, I had purposely narrowed my universe of potential customers to an infinitesimal number—just CEOs and people of similar rank. I might as well have limited my job to being a heart surgeon who only repaired aortic valves in left-handed men in New Hampshire. But the more I stuck to this narrow job description, the better I got at it, until there was a day that I could legitimately say my one trick—helping successful executives achieve lasting behavioral change—was now my "genius." Not many people were doing this thirty years ago. Not only had I created a unique job suited to my limited interests and skills, but for a while there, I practically had the field all to myself. I had created a life I could literally call my own.*

When that happens, the world beats a path to your door. And that, I'm convinced, dramatically improves your odds of living a life in which fulfillment overwhelms regret. You've created a virtuous circle in which you're doing what you were meant to do, you're good at it, people recognize you for it and seek you out, and you're constantly improving. It's an enviable position to attain, the essence of an earned achievement. You've become what I like to call a "one-trick genius."

I'm using "genius" liberally here, referring to anyone whose dedication to being excellent in their narrow area of expertise is immediately manifest to friends and strangers alike. For example, I was visiting New York and chipped a tooth before a breakfast meeting. I was in pain throughout the meeting, urgently in need of a dentist. My host, seeing my anguish, insisted that I see his dentist in Rockefeller Center that day—and set up an appointment for me while we were at the table. "He'll take care of you," the host assured me. "He's a genius." I'd heard hyperbolic recommendations like this before. Everyone thinks *their* doctor, nanny, plumber, massage therapist is the world-class wizard who can solve your problem. In this case, my host was right. From the moment I stepped into the office, where the receptionist greeted me by name before I said a word, to the hygienist who cleaned my teeth, to the state-of-the-art equipment the dentist used to treat me and his solicitous manner

---

* I'd like to say I had this career strategy fully thought out. Not true. I needed time to appreciate that (a) the issues CEOs face are more consequential than those of the average executive and are therefore more engaging and (b) the fees are better at the top.

in making sure he didn't add to my pain, I knew I was in the hands of a master healer who took pride in his expertise.

If you've grown up in a community where Main Street has more than three traffic lights, you know people like that dentist. They're the local craftsmen and attorneys and teachers and doctors and coaches who immediately impress you with their hypercompetence in their chosen field. I regard all of them as one-trick geniuses (or OTG for short). They're the kind of people the Nobel Prize–winning physicist and teacher Richard Feynman had in mind when he advised his students:

> *Fall in love with some activity, and do it! Nearly everything is really interesting if you go into it deeply enough. Work as hard and as much as you want to on the things you like to do the best. Don't think about what you want to be, but what you want to do. Keep up some kind of a minimum with other things so that society doesn't stop you from doing anything at all.*

I cannot tell you what kind of "specialist" or OTG to be. The clients and friends who've attained OTG status in my eyes are a varied lot, but with few exceptions, they employed some or all of the following five strategies to find their "genius":

1. FINDING YOUR GENIUS TAKES TIME

Few people know their position on the generalist versus specialist debate at the start of their career. Like me, they're too young. They don't have the try-this, try-that experience yet. Even fewer know what their "genius" is. It's a process that takes at least a decade or two of adulthood to resolve. I've heard this time period referred to as the "exposure gap." From a running start with your acquired base of knowledge and ability, you steadily *expose* yourself to new sets of people, experience, and ideas. You add skills that work in your favor and subtract those that don't. Eventually you narrow down to the pursuit most likely to engage and fulfill you. It was true for me, but a more vivid example is Sandy Ogg. He not only became a specialist late in his career, but his particular genius happens to be identifying other specialists, especially the ones who add the most value to an organization.

I met Sandy Ogg in grad school, when we worked next to each other in Professor Paul Hersey's office. Sandy went into corporate human resources where he rapidly rose to become HR chief at Motorola's largest division. In 2003, he took the same position at the giant consumer goods company Unilever. By then Sandy was in his midforties and an expert on all the customary aspects of HR—training, development, benefits, compensation, diversity, and the rest. But Unilever's CEO told Sandy to delegate those duties to lieutenants. He wanted Sandy to formalize a way to identify Unilever's future leaders. The challenge engaged Sandy completely. Within a short time he developed a methodology that measured what he called Talent to Value. Analyzing Unilever's three hundred thousand employees through a proprietary formula, he concluded that just fifty-six people at Unilever were responsible for 90 percent of its value.

My definition of brilliant is having an idea that no one has thought of before yet sounds obvious the moment you hear it. Sandy's insight was so brilliant and had such a positive impact on Unilever's stock price that the private equity powerhouse Blackstone hired him away to conduct similar analyses of who was adding the most value at Blackstone's portfolio companies. Sandy learned that there is low correlation between a top manager's compensation and the value he or she adds. His insight uncovered a data point every CEO would love to know about an organization: *Who is overpaid, who is underpaid.* It was especially insightful at a private equity firm, where investments are made with leveraged money, dramatically increasing the importance of a proper valuation when you sell an asset. Each dollar you receive in the sale might represent ten times your original investment. Sandy's equations not only identified the people worth keeping and the managers to let go, but he also concluded that some people were so valuable that, given the outsized returns for success in private equity, no amount of compensation was too high. These people, Sandy also learned, were invariably specialists—and their value was embedded in that term: They were "special." Pay them whatever it takes to keep them, he said.

When Sandy does a deep dive for undervalued talent at a company, he's invariably searching for the specialists management is ignoring. They're rarely the leadership class of generalists showing up at the weekly senior management meeting. Typically, he interviews people up and down the organization about their peers, noting the one or two names repeatedly praised as superstars. On one assignment he kept hearing the company's head of procurement described in glowing terms. When he made his initial report to the CEO, he asked, "Tell me the ten most important jobs here."

The CEO started with himself, then went down his pyramid of direct reports.

"What about the head of procurement?" Sandy asked.

The CEO went blank.

"Do you know who your head of procurement is?"

The CEO had no idea.

Sandy explained that he should probably get to know this fellow because he had a gift for saving the company money. Sandy knew the specific amount. "Lose him," he said, "and you've got a six-hundred-million-dollar hole in your value agenda."

Sandy was revealing the complete disconnect between the role that adds huge value to a company and the investment in terms of training, compensation, and grooming that the company makes in the person filling that role. In Sandy's opinion, that person is almost always a specialist, sometimes overlooked and underappreciated, but not for long.

Sandy is my ideal of a "one-trick genius." Starting with the broad knowledge of a human resources professional, he narrowed his focus to determining one particular data point of interest to top management. Who's overpaid, who's underpaid? Then he whittled it down to one question that CEOs didn't even know they should be asking: Who in the organization can never be overpaid? The delicious irony here is that when Sandy identifies the value creators at a company, he's identifying someone just like him: a specialist doing a job so valuable that he or she cannot be commodified or replaced. He is *the* expert on the concept of one-trick genius.

Remember this the next time you wonder why it's taking you so long to identify a job or career that fully engages and fulfills you. You need years, not months, of experience to develop the knowledge base, the work habits, and the relationships that will enable you to slice the loaf down to a single sliver of expertise that is yours to own. And, to further torture the metaphor, you have to let the loaf bake fully before you can slice it.

2. THE RIGHT TALENT CANNOT SHINE IN THE WRONG ROLE

When Sandy Ogg first tried to link talent to value at Unilever, he discovered that he was overlooking an important ingredient, namely, the role people were being asked to assume. If you have talented people in the wrong role, their talent is wasted and they will fail. No amount of talent can overcome an inappropriate role.

Sandy's insight was that Unilever didn't have fifty-six people out of three hundred thousand employees who contributed 90 percent of the value at the company. Actually, it had fifty-six *roles* making that outsized contribution, and his job was to sync each of those roles with the right person. When that happened, he could feel a "click," as if he were locking his seatbelt. Failure to click was failure to create value.

It's the same in an individual life. Each of us assumes various roles in life: partner, colleague, parent, friend, sibling, son, daughter. We intuitively know that the behavior we display in one role is not necessarily productive in another role, which is one reason we don't talk to our spouse the way we talk to a direct report. But being in sync with our role requires more from us. Are we adding value in each of those relationships? Do our efforts to add value in the role align with our abilities? And finally, does the role matter to us? Is it something we gladly put on when we wake up each morning, not grudgingly accept because we have no other options? When the three answers align at yes, we have a much better chance of finding our OTG.

3. A ONE-TRICK GENIUS IS NOT A ONE-TRICK PONY

Do not confuse "one-trick genius" with the pejorative "one-trick pony." The term "one-trick pony" is judgmental and denigrating, referring to people who abuse a limited skill set—whether it's the same predictable response to every situation or one slick move on the basketball court—because they have no choice. It's all they've got.

OTG, by contrast, is a deeply considered choice, representing what we aspire to rather than what we settle for. We rummage around our toolkit, discarding the skills that lack the potential for excellence and zeroing in on a talent we wouldn't mind perfecting over a lifetime.

The specific talent—your one trick—doesn't matter as much as the sincere attempt to perfect it does. In that sense, anyone can be a one-trick genius. You don't have to be supernaturally gifted like a math, music, or tennis prodigy to earn the OTG title. The best sushi chef in town is a one-trick genius (the chef's "one trick" is working with the lone ingredient of raw fish; the "genius" is demonstrating that raw fish doesn't limit the chef at all). So is the busiest bankruptcy lawyer, and the always booked haircutter, and the high school choirmaster whose singers perennially win the state championship. Odds are high that, given the internal and external validation that goes along with being the best in town, each has found fulfillment in his or her OTG.

4. YOUR UNIQUENESS CAN BE YOUR GENIUS

Betsy Wills, founder of YouScience, an aptitude testing firm in Nashville, suggests that, as possible sources of our "genius," we examine not only the inclinations and habits that delight us but the ones that frustrate us as well. She observed this in the career choice of her husband, Ridley Wills. In his teens, Ridley developed an eye for aesthetic order and refinement. His maternal grandfather was an architect and his father was a historic preservation scholar, so Ridley was well versed in the building trades. He could discern the difference between thirty shades of blue. He could tell when a carpenter's handiwork was not level. If something was off in the design or construction of a building, not only could he see it immediately, but he'd want to fix it. The same with an untidy room; he'd have to clean it up. This was his gift and his curse— a maddening, exhausting way to live.

Things didn't get better during Ridley's first two years of college, until he realized he was meant to be an architect. He transferred from Stanford to the University of Virginia for its strong architecture faculty and beautiful neoclassical campus. After college, he set up his own shop back home in Nashville, where he quickly established himself as the city's top residential design-and-build firm. In his midthirties, he participated in a research project matching psychological profiles and careers. After two days of testing, the researchers concluded that Ridley had a very powerful sense of "pitch discrimination." It was similar to a musician with perfect pitch for musical notes or a wine sommelier with a perfect nose. In Ridley's case, he applied his pitch discrimination to design, constantly perceiving tiny distinctions in the quality and beauty of a home. The researchers, unaware of Ridley's profession, told him he was best suited for work that required precision, attention to detail, and highly refined aesthetic discernment. They suggested he become either a fine art photographer or a high-end home renovation specialist.

"Most of us are satisfied delivering work that's ninety percent of perfect," Betsy told me. "My husband aims for ninety-nine percent. Somehow he chose the one field where he could release that ninety-nine percent compulsion and be happy rather than miserable."

This wasn't the first time I'd heard a potential source of misery evolving into an individual's OTG. Years earlier I had met a man at a dinner party who could tell me what was being prepared for dinner in the kitchen two rooms away. He claimed to have such a keen sense of smell that he could detect mental illness (evidently caused by a metabolic flaw, particularly in schizophrenics). When a mentally ill person boarded a bus in his hometown of Amsterdam, he'd immediately get off the bus to escape the noxious odor.

"That would be a very valuable talent for a mental health professional," I said. "Is that what you do back in Amsterdam?"

"No, that would be hell for me," he said. "I'm a *parfumier*. I custom-blend perfumes for wealthy people who want their own signature scent."

"There's a living in that?" I asked.

"People will always want to smell good. I make them happy."

A special talent can elevate or torment you. You can let it be your ally or your nemesis. It's your choice.

5. GENERALISTS CAN BE OTGs TOO

At first glance, CEOs appear to be the ultimate generalists. But peel away the necessary but generalized leadership skills of clear communication, persuasion, and decision making, and you'll find that every good CEO has a very specific skill or core value that they regard as their OTG. One CEO's OTG might be running a productive meeting; another's might be creating total alignment at every level of the organization. The genius in each CEO's trick is that this isolated skill is the foundation of the CEO's credibility and respect; it governs everything.

This specialist quality isn't always apparent in great leaders, perhaps masked by their heavy authority and big personalities. But it's there if you look long enough. For example, I read an admiring profile of my great friend Frances Hesselbein in David Epstein's 2019 bestseller *Range: Why Generalists Triumph in a Specialized World*, a book whose thesis (and subtitle) would seem to contradict the argument I'm making here. Epstein provides a nicely detailed account of Frances's greatness—her early years as a busy volunteer, how in her sixties and seventies she revived the Girl Scouts, and the Presidential Medal of Freedom that Bill Clinton awarded her, and Peter Drucker's assertion that she was the best CEO in America—presumably making the case that Frances's distinguishing leadership skill is her wide-ranging background. Yet he doesn't quite manage to put his finger on the one skill that actually sets Frances apart. Frances sees everything through the prism of one question: How can I be of service to others? It's her "genius" through which all her formidable strengths of wisdom, authority, integrity, and compassion flow. It is how Frances makes others see the world her way. It is how she leads.

For example, in 2014 I invited a half dozen clients to my home in San Diego for an intense two-day session to help each person figure out what they wanted to do next. I also invited Frances, who was ninety-eight at the time, knowing her presence would automatically raise the wisdom level in the room. On the second day, our attention turned to a woman I'll call Rose Anne, not yet fifty, who had sold her business three years earlier for a healthy sum and moved with her husband from Minneapolis to a small town in Arizona to enjoy the fruits of her labors. The move had been disastrous. Rose Anne wasn't built for gazing at Arizona sunsets. The restless entrepreneur in her invested in a local restaurant and a fitness club, customer-facing businesses that were vastly different from how she had made her original fortune. Within a year, as she applied her hard-nosed business skills in the town, she managed to alienate everyone she met, so much so that her husband threatened to move back to Minneapolis if she didn't make it right. As she sang her tale of woe in my home, we made suggestions, none very helpful—until Frances, who spoke last. She told Rose Anne, "It seems to me that you've been thinking a lot about serving yourself. Perhaps you should try helping others." All of us knew she was right. Even Rose Anne, lost in her despair, nodded in agreement and thanked Frances. All Frances needed were two pithy sentences, obvious to all of us the moment they were uttered, to give Rose Anne a path to turn her life around. That is her OTG. Frances lives to serve others and her example persuades strangers to follow her lead. Her authority stems from this single attribute, not the other way around. At heart, she is a specialist masquerading as a generalist. Five years later, Rose Anne ran for mayor—and won.

By the way, I'm not deriding Epstein's book. *Range* is fascinating, well argued, and rich in detail. If I read him correctly, Epstein is arguing *in favor of* later-in-life specialization, the kind that comes after we've sampled many disciplines and settled on the one worthy of our laser-like focus. I believe we're saying the same thing: If we're lucky, we begin as generalists, end up as specialists.

THE LIFE OF an artisan—a serious craftsman committed to doing a worthwhile task as well as it can be done—is my image of a one-trick genius at work. It suggests a career that you regard as a calling rather than a job, pursued more for personal fulfillment than a paycheck. This is the benefit of being an OTG: When you feel fulfilled, your world expands rather than constricts. You discover that your narrow expertise can be applied to an ever wider array of problems and opportunities. OTG is not an insult that sentences you to a shrunken, one-dimensional life. To the contrary, when you develop a highly specialized skill and practice it like a dedicated craftsman, you can call the shots. You're more unique and therefore in greater demand. You're more engaged and blessed with greater purpose. You are checking all the boxes of fulfillment and, in turn, living your own life.

EXERCISE

How to Hear the "You Can Be More" Speech

Curtis Martin described for me one of the most significant moments in his NFL career. It happened at the New England Patriots training camp in 1996 after Curtis's rookie season when he had led the American Conference with 1,487 yards rushing. Head coach Bill Parcells, a legendary motivator, gathered all the running backs and receivers for a last-man-standing endurance test of sprints and drills. As exhausted players started dropping out after fifty minutes, Curtis was determined not to quit before Parcells blew the whistle. An hour later, he was the only player left on the field, finishing sprints on hands and knees but refusing to be broken until Parcells mercifully ended the session. Afterward, in the locker room, Parcells told Curtis, "I did that because I wanted you to learn this about yourself: *You can be so much more.*"

Curtis's story reminded me that each of us has been hearing some variation of the You Can Be More (or YCBM for short) speech all our lives. I'm sure you're familiar with it too. In one form or another it was an essential component of your parent's cheerleading repertoire whenever they were enthralled with you ("I'm proud of you . . .") or disappointed ("I expect more from you . . .").

It's a speech you need to hear at regular intervals in your life. Unfortunately, it's also a speech that is dropped so casually into conversation—in many guises—that it might sail over your head. There's rarely a blaring alarm announcing that a YCBM missile is coming your way.

The YCBM speech as *assignment* was what Sandy Ogg was hearing when Unilever's CEO asked him to identify the company's valuable talent. The speech took the form of a *frustrated outburst* when I shouted at Mark Tercek, "Dammit, when are you going to start living your own life?" It was phrased as a *question* when Ayse Birsel asked me, "Who are your heroes?" Fortunately, in all three cases, the YCBM message eventually came through loud and clear. It changed three people's lives—Sandy's, Mark's, and mine.

Each of the half dozen or so pivotal moments in my life—moments that brought me closer to my OTG—were instigated by an unsolicited and unexpected YCBM speech: Paul Hersey asking me to fill in for him at a lecture, assuring me that I could pull it off; the head of American Express telling me I'd be better off working for myself, without a senior partner; a literary agent from New York tracking me down to say, "You should write a book." These are only some of the times I've been on the receiving end of the YCBM message. Who knows how often I missed equivalent messages because I wasn't paying attention?

DO THIS: For an extended period of time—a month at least—keep a log of every time someone says something to you that sounds as if they see latent potential that you have been overlooking. It can be specific praise ("That was a good point you made in the meeting. It never occurred to me"). Or an open-ended suggestion ("You should be more assertive"). Or tough love ("Do it over. I expected better from you"). This isn't a test on which you can be right or wrong about the comment's meaning. The goal here is to open your eyes and ears to how often people are communicating that they see something promising or undeveloped in you that you should exploit. You're not just looking for praise. You're looking for insights about how you can be better.

The compliments, whether meaningful or empty, should be easy to spot (we excel at tracking praise directed our way). It might be tougher to track the on-point critiques and brutally honest asides, although my hunch is they cut the deepest and contain the most actionable advice.* Keeping a meticulous log elevates awareness and appreciation—always.

---

* A banker once told me that the turning point in his young career was instigated by a You Can Be More speech disguised as an offhanded insult. I asked him to put it in writing:

"Early in my career, in the late '70s, I approached the CEO of an iconic American conglomerate with a very creative refinancing idea that could save his company a lot of money. It took me nearly two years to get the CEO on board and then pull off the deal, during which I updated him from time to time when something major came up. He was a busy man who I didn't want to bother. I wouldn't say we were friends—he was a titan, I was a pipsqueak—but he'd call me out of the blue some times and we'd have these odd conversations about politics or sports, rarely about the deal, after which I'd ask myself, 'What was that about?' Given our vastly different ranks, I had a hard time accepting that we could ever be buddies.

"A few days after we closed the deal, I arranged a meeting between him and my bank's chairman to celebrate. Just the three of us in his office clinking champagne glasses. The two of them were in a jolly mood. The deal had dazzled my client's board members and earned a big fee for the bank. Then they did something remarkable. They started talking about me as if I wasn't there. They joked about my youth (I was 29) and how I owed them my career. Then the CEO told my chairman his frank opinion of me. The words still ring in my ears. He said I was 'creative and a great negotiator' but I was also an 'unmade bed.' He was smiling as he said this, but he wasn't joking. He wanted me to hear it. He didn't elaborate. The conversation turned to other things, but he had delivered the intended jab and left a bruise.

"I thought about that 'unmade bed' comment for days. How had I displeased him? I couldn't come up with any lapses in the paperwork and legal filings. Then I recalled all those times he'd call to shoot the breeze, how I couldn't wait to get him off the phone out of fear that I was wasting his

For extra credit, also log those moments when you are offering rather than receiving the YCBM message—when you are volunteering feedback to make someone else a little better. You might be doing it more than you realize. This is a good thing. The YCBM message is one of the purest forms of generosity we have in life. It is good medicine for both giver and taker. As the poet Maggie Smith says, "Shine on someone else—the light will reach you, too."

time. I didn't appreciate that he found gratification in helping me succeed. The unscheduled phone calls were his way of fostering trust and sealing our friendship. He was signaling that there's more to business than creativity and deal making. If I ignored the human element—especially the reciprocal part, such as the satisfaction of helping someone and letting them experience the satisfaction of helping you back—then I was missing the stuff that made work emotionally gratifying. Basically, he was saying that I could have done a much better job of hand-holding a client. I never made that mistake again."

EXERCISE

The One-Trick Genius Roundtable

This one's provocative but fun.

DO THIS: Gather six people in your living room who know one another well. Starting with yourself, identify the one skill that you believe is your special talent, the hidden or self-evident one-trick genius that makes you most effective. Each of the other five people must then respond. No one gets a pass. If they disagree with you, they must offer an alternative opinion. Repeat the process with each member of the group.

Feel free to debate any comment. Cynicism and meanness are forbidden, as are anger and hostility at anyone for being honest. Thirty-six opinions of agreement or disagreement will be expressed in your group, but no one is allowed to be disagreeable.

There will be flattery and pain and surprise. But this is not an exercise in self-congratulation or self-flagellation. Like YCBM, it's about self-awareness and helping one another. The first time I tried this, I confidently asserted that my unique talent was understanding other people's motivations before they did. I've believed this about myself since my twenties, after three years of leading intense encounter groups at UCLA (a midcentury phenomenon in which participants were encouraged to express feelings, often in confrontational encounters). None of the people disagreed that I had this talent, but it didn't make me unique. Several people also felt they were excellent at spotting others' motivation. The most accurate observation, from a woman I've been coaching for a dozen years, was more mundane. My gift, she said, was not getting bored by repetitive activity, such as delivering my message more than one hundred times a year with the same level of enthusiasm. "Lots of people understand motivation," she said. "Not many can stay on message." Until she said it, I'd never regarded that ability as anything special. My only response was "Thank you."

Part II

EARNING
YOUR LIFE

CHAPTER 8

HOW WE EARN: THE FIVE BUILDING BLOCKS OF DISCIPLINE

———————

As we begin this new section, let's review where we've been. In the introduction we asserted that *we are living an earned life when the choices, risks, and effort we make in each moment align with an overarching purpose in our lives, regardless of the eventual outcome.* Each chapter focused on one facet of the mindset required to achieve an earned life. We kicked off with the Every Breath Paradigm about our sense of self, based on Buddha's teaching, "Every breath I take is a new me." Then we reviewed the many forces that compel us to live lives other than our own. We countered those with a checklist of skills essential to an earned life (motivation, ability, understanding, confidence, support, and marketplace). Then a chapter on the value of reducing the major choices in our life from many options to one, followed by a chapter on aspiration, noting that there's a crucial difference between deciding what we want to be and who we want to become. In chapter 6, we examined how we determine the level of risk we're willing to accept in our life. Finally, in chapter 7, I urged you to choose a specialist when it's time to resolve the eternal specialist-versus-generalist dichotomy. On every page, the persistent unifying theme has been choosing—how to refine our choices so that they serve rather than sabotage us.

In part 2, we will be focusing on the actions, rather than the mindset, required to live an earned life. It is a challenge that demands a new framework for how you execute your choices and get things done.

The traditional paradigm for achieving any goal emphasizes discipline and willpower. If we want to succeed, we must (a) religiously follow our plan and (b) resist any distraction that tempts us off plan. Discipline supplies the power to say yes every day to doing the hard stuff. Willpower provides the determination to say no to the bad stuff. We admire, often to the point of amazement, anyone who displays these two virtues to accomplish something difficult or extraordinary: the sibling who loses sixty pounds and keeps them off; the neighbor who accomplishes her lifelong dream of fluency in Italian; the addict who kicks the habit.

But in our own lives, we're not so admirable or worthy of other people's amazement. Of all the personal qualities we overestimate in ourselves—our intelligence, our discretion, our driving skill, our willingness to take criticism, our punctuality, our wit, to name a few—discipline and willpower probably rank first. We've got the failed diets and unused gym memberships and uncracked foreign language primers to prove it.

I stopped overestimating my discipline in my early thirties (admitting this failing was a point of pride for me). Yet I did not extend this insight to the people I was training back then; time and time again I continued to overestimate their discipline. I needed a client stumping me with an obvious question to open my eyes. In 1990 I was doing a series of "Values and Leadership" seminars at Northrop Corporation, the aerospace and defense company now known as Northrop Grumman. After one of the all-day sessions, Kent Kresa, Northrop's plainspoken, newly minted CEO, who was just beginning the company's spectacular turnaround from near bankruptcy to most admired status, asked me, "Does this stuff actually work?"

My first impulse, wholly self-justifying, was to say "Of course." But no one had ever asked me this question before.

"I think so," I said. "But I haven't done any research to prove it works. So I guess I don't know. I'll find out."

In my training classes, I instruct leaders to follow up regularly with their team to get feedback from their co-workers on how they're doing with what they learned in the classroom, assuming that they would comply with my instructions. Seeking feedback on our activity is a proven way of regulating and improving our performance in that activity. But I'd never followed up to see whether they actually took my instruction to heart.

It's no mystery why I hadn't questioned the efficacy of my training program: I was afraid of the answer. Better to put my head in the sand and assume the best. After Kresa's probing question, I changed my ways. Northrop's HR team and I polled the leaders who had participated in the training classes each month to see if they were following up on their learning with their co-workers. After several months, the numbers were encouraging. The more we checked in on the participants, the better they got at seeking feedback on their management skills from their co-workers. Our follow-up served as a steady reminder to the participants that they'd spent a day in a classroom with a workbook of strategies they were expected to digest and practice. Combined with the implicit message that management was paying attention, it prodded them to get better at seeking feedback and, as a result, at applying what they learned in class.

A few months later I was ready to answer Kresa's question: "Yes, people get better, but only with follow-up."

"Young man," he said, "I just made your career."

He was right (his question was yet another life-changing You Can Be More episode for me). From that moment, follow-up in all its incarnations became an essential component in my thinking and coaching. Until then, I had been relying on individual motivation and discipline to drive people to follow my instruction. I thought, "I teach it; it's up to the students to learn it and use it." This was insanity, of course—contradicting centuries of evidence that human beings are very poor at any form of self-regulation. I had been cured by Kent Kresa's basic question: *Does this stuff actually work?*

I learned that follow-up works in altering our behavior, but it was not effective on its own. It had to be combined with several other actions in order to instill the motivation, energy, and self-regulation that we have come to think of as discipline and willpower.

This new template of actions offers a reinterpretation of discipline and willpower in our life. We tend to think of these two noble but overgeneralized attributes as the essential skills that deliver success. I suggest they are not. Rather, they are the *evidence* of our success, qualities we only recognize after the fact. In a gross oversimplification, we label them as discipline and willpower (or grit, resilience, perseverance, stick-to-itiveness, pluck, spine, tenacity, moral fiber, determination, and so on). Concepts so unique and precise should not have that many synonyms. The building blocks of "discipline" and "willpower" are much more concrete and comprehensible:

- Compliance
- Accountability

- Follow-up
- Measurement

These four actions are not surrogates for discipline and will-power; they're replacements sprinting onto the field as part of a new game plan. Each of the four actions is situational: compliance resolves a different problem than accountability or follow-up or measurement. We call on one or the other at different moments in the earning process. Together they become your template for structuring your pursuit of any goal. You're probably already practicing them, albeit inconsistently. If you want to live an earned life, they work. Without them, you don't stand a chance. Here's why.

1. COMPLIANCE

Compliance reflects your adherence to an external policy or rule. You hear it most commonly applied in the context of medical treatment. Your doctor prescribes medication, and your only task is to take the medication on schedule. You're not being ordered to do anything extraordinary. Just follow the instructions and you'll get better. Yet an estimated 50 percent of all U.S. patients either forget, abandon, or never take the medication. That's how tough compliance is. Even when our health, possibly our life, hangs in the balance, we don't comply with a surefire remedy.

When I was twenty-four, I mangled the middle finger of my right hand catching a hard pass in a basketball game. The top third of the finger dangled loosely from the rest of my hand like a broken tree limb. I researched the injury in the library, learning that I probably had "baseball finger." The treatment was simple but tedious. I needed to wear a splint for eight weeks, even in the

shower, after which I had to wash and dry my finger on a flat sur-
face to make sure I didn't re-stretch the tendon and undo the healing process. When I described my research findings to the UCLA
clinic doctor, he said, "That's right. Baseball finger. Just follow the
splinting procedure and see me in twelve weeks. You should be
fine then."

My compliance was total. I washed, dried, and re-splinted my
finger with the devotion of a mother changing a newborn's diaper.
On my return eight weeks later, the doctor examined my finger and
declared it healed. Then he added, "I am impressed that you actually followed through. Very few patients do this for twelve weeks."

This was one of the more disappointing statements I'd heard
from a doctor. He had diagnosed my problem and offered the correct therapy, but he'd made no effort to warn me that adhering to
the steps would be difficult, or that he expected me to fail utterly.
Compliance was up to me, and he had not been optimistic. It was
as if he had sent me on a journey by car on a route that had no stop
signs, no speed limits, and no warning signs announcing "Steep
Hill Ahead" or "Dangerous Curve."

It reminded me that Hippocrates famously exhorted physi-
cians, "First do no harm." But he also urged them "to make the
patient cooperate." Not only did my doctor expect me to fail at
compliance, but he was failing to comply with Hippocrates' edict.
Sadly, he remains the rule rather than the exception. Patient non-
compliance remains a $100-billion-a-year cost item in American
medicine. Raise your hand if your doctor has ever checked with
the pharmacy to see if you actually picked up your prescription,
or called you a week or two after your visit to make sure you were
taking your medication.

The doctor was right, of course. Compliance is easy to understand ("If I comply, I get better"), but hard to do ("I have to do it every day. Ugh!"). Humans are woefully bad at compliance, whether we're flouting our doctors' recommendations, our teachers' summer reading lists or nightly homework assignments, our parents' requests to make our beds, or our editors' deadlines. I only wish he'd felt a little responsibility to warn his patients of that.

Here's a simple truth: You can't count on the people issuing the orders to hold your hand to ensure compliance. You're on your own. Nor can you count on every situation to compel compliance. I completed the splint therapy only because I was in pain and I didn't want a crippled hand for the rest of my life. Absent the pain and disfigured hand, I doubt I would have been so compliant.

The baseball finger incident taught me this: We're more likely to comply with a recommended course of action when failure to do so results in extreme pain or punishment, either physical, financial, or emotional. Your health doesn't improve. Your injury doesn't heal. You lose your job. Your relationship founders. You suffer long-lasting regret for an opportunity squandered.

When you're faced with one of those extreme situations that threaten you with existential pain or punishment—and you recognize the seriousness of the moment—compliance should not be a challenge. You have no other choice. For other situations, you might need a different tactic.

2. ACCOUNTABILITY

Unlike compliance, which is our productive response to the expectations imposed on us by other people, *accountability* is our response to expectations we impose on ourselves. Our sense of accountability comes in two models: private or public.

The to-do list is a common example of private accountability. We scribble our daily to-do items on a yellow pad or type them into our mobile phone, then cross them out as we go through our day. Each cross-out is a small private victory. If we only get through half our list, we carry over the undone items to the next day. If some of them remain undone a week later, the frustration or shame is ours alone. No one else needs to know.

I prefer public disclosure. When your intentions are out in the open, the stakes are automatically higher (people are watching) and so, hopefully, is your performance. The specter of a public setback, coupled with your private disappointment, is a powerful motivator. This is one reason I insist that my coaching clients fully advertise their plans to change their behavior to the people they work with: disclosure makes the effort to change visible; visibility elevates accountability.

3. FOLLOW-UP

Compliance and accountability are two sides of the same coin. They're both burdens that we bear alone as individuals, one imposed on us by others, the other self-imposed. *Follow-up* introduces the coercive force of the outside world to the mix. Suddenly, other people are checking up on us, taking an interest in our opinions and valuing our feedback. We are no longer acting as sole proprietors of our life. We have been conscripted into a group for the purpose of being observed and tested and judged. And that conscription alters us. Like it or not, follow-up is a valuable process that heightens our self-awareness. It forces us to assess our progress honestly. Without follow-up we may never take the time to ask how we're doing.

Follow-up appears in many forms. It could be someone from HR conducting a company-wide survey, or our boss requesting a weekly progress report, or a vendor checking to see if we're satisfied with a purchase. The specific kind of follow-up I'll be recommending in subsequent chapters, derived from the Business Plan Review at Ford, is a weekly group meeting created by a half dozen or so participants to monitor one another. Whatever form our follow-up takes, we should welcome it rather than resent it. It's a supportive gesture, not an intrusion on our integrity and personal space.

4. MEASUREMENT

Measurement is the truest indicator of our priorities—because what we measure drives out what we don't. If financial security is your top priority, you check your net worth every day. If you're serious about losing weight, you step on a scale each morning. If you have stomach issues, you measure the composition of your gut biome. In 2020, if COVID-19 was your daily fear, you might have taken to using a tiny device called an oximeter to measure your SpO_2 levels (aka blood oxygen), a data point you probably had never heard of the year before.

I'm not a card-carrying member of the Quantified Self movement, a burgeoning community of scientists and tech wizards who aim to find private meaning by measuring all manner of personal data, from daily steps to weekly minutes spent socializing. But in years past, when it mattered to me, I've tracked hours slept, days away from home, times I told my kids I loved them, daily moments of gratitude, and Michelin-starred restaurants visited. Each number helped me improve, and in many cases I stopped tracking when I reached "good enough." For many years I obsessively tracked airline miles; I stopped counting and declared victory the moment I hit ten million miles and received my American Airlines ConciergeKey card. As I write this, I'm tracking daily steps, kind words to Lyda, daily minutes of quiet reflection, face time with the grandkids, how much white food (sugar, pasta, potatoes) I eat, and daily minutes spent on low-priority activities (e.g. watching TV).

Not every measurement that matters to us has to be a hard, objective number. Soft, subjective numbers can be just as meaningful.

Consider my friend Scott who went on a strict doctor-supervised diet for a medical condition. Six months into the diet, Scott's internist (who had adopted the diet himself as a preventive measure for the same condition) asked him to estimate how well he'd adhered to the strict diet. Scott said, "Ninety-eight point five percent." The internist said nothing and moved on to the next question. The lack of feedback irked Scott. The next day he called the internist to say, "When I said ninety-eight point five percent, I felt you were judging me harshly."

"Not at all," said the internist. "I was impressed. I'm no better than eighty percent." Hearing another measurement to compare against his own, imprecise as it may have been, was instantly meaningful to Scott. It made him feel better about his level of compliance.

The measurement we'll be asking you to make in the next chapter is also a soft, subjective number. You'll be estimating your level of effort on a scale of 1 to 10. Your 6's and 9's will be no more scientific than Scott's 98.5 percent—they're estimates, after all—but in the context of pursuing an earned life, they'll carry a world of meaning for you, especially when you can compare your numbers with other people's.

AS YOU START implementing the strategies for living a no-regrets life, these four components of the earning template will become second nature to you. Compliance and accountability will cease to be daily tests of your shaky commitment—as if you have a choice between doing the work and taking a day off. They will evolve into autonomic responses, like your heartbeat or your breathing. Follow-up and measurement will be the feedback loops that give meaning and purpose to your day. You will insist on the data rather than cover your eyes and ears. This is how discipline and willpower gradually settle into your life. They're not bequeathed to you at birth. You earn them every day.

BUT THERE IS one more component that binds these four actions together. And it is a big one that's already staring you in the face. It comprises all the people in your life. It is the domain you think of as your *community*.

You may think of yourself as a wholly self-made rugged individualist who takes responsibility for choices made, never whines "It's not fair!" and always rejects the role of victim or martyr. I've met admirable people who embody all these traits but one: *None of them believes they are wholly self-made.* They know that an earned life cannot be achieved in isolation. It only thrives within a community.

Not only do they appreciate that their choices and aspirations affect other people (it's one of the first lessons in Humanity 101:

"No man is an island," and all that), but they never lose sight of the fact that a community is not all one-way streets. Everything is reciprocal in a community. Much of the good that you do for others without expectation of payback—comforting them, following up with them, connecting them to someone, or simply being present and hearing them—comes back to you whether you seek it or not, because reciprocity is a defining feature of community.

But in a community, this reciprocity is not merely the two-dimensional kind between two individuals. In the right kind of community it's three-dimensional—as if everyone has a license to help and coach anyone else at any time. It's not the transactional I'll-scratch-your-back-if-you-scratch-mine reciprocity of aggressive networking. It happens when someone says "I need help." And someone else, without making a "What's-in-it-for-me?" calculation, hears the plea and responds, "I can help." In healthy communities, "I can help" is the default response. If you were to chart the crisscrossing lines of communication and generous acts among members of a healthy community, it would look as wild and random as a Jackson Pollock drip painting or a map of our nervous system.

I did not fully appreciate this phenomenon until I was nearing seventy and woke up one morning to discover that, by accident, I had created a community of my own—my 100 Coaches project—and that it was a force multiplier in helping people live an earned life. How I arrived at this new place is still a miracle to me, with an origin story worth telling.

CHAPTER 9

AN ORIGIN STORY

Y ou already know what to do to achieve an earned life: *Decide what you want that life to look like, then work as hard as necessary to make your decision come true.*

No one but you can paint that vision. The influential people in your life, with their opinions and nudges, may offer the intellectual and emotional tools to help you choose a wise path. But in the end, the choice, whether rendered early on or after years of false starts, is yours alone to make.

As for the hard work part, that's a challenge overcome by the application of structure. Structure is how we tame the unruly impulses that lure us away from achieving our goals. Structure is the most effective tool we have to repair and renew our lives, and unlike deciding what life path to take, structure can easily be adopted or inspired thanks to others.* If we can't provide the appropriate

---

*Structure is particularly useful with the small stuff. A friend once mocked me for tracking how many times I said something nice to my wife each day. "You shouldn't have to be reminded to be nice to your wife," he said.

"Evidently I do," I said. "I'm not ashamed that I need a reminder to behave better. It would be shameful if I knew it and didn't do anything about it."

That's the power of imposing structure. Structure reminds us not to relax our standards, especially the small but necessary gestures that we take for granted. My friend now keeps a daily log of how many times he asks his wife, "How can I help?"

structure to ourselves, we seek out sources that can, whether it's a personal trainer to implement our fitness regime, a boss to set our job's agenda, or a book offering a plan to declutter our home.

My business card could legitimately say STRUCTURE CONSUL-TANT under my name. That's what I do. I peel away the outer skin of a behavioral problem to examine the infrastructure, then reframe the infrastructure to address the *real* problem.

I gleefully confess that I do not suffer from Not-Invented-Here syndrome. I'm a connoisseur of other people's ideas, and when I hear a workable idea created by someone else, I internalize it as my own. The value I add is taking the idea and folding it with other ideas into a structure that works for me and my clients. The Life Plan Review, or LPR for short, that we cover in chapter 10 is such a structure. It's the book's major action point: a weekly check-in format for achieving meaningful change and leading an earned life. It's the end product of my attempt to add intelligible structure in one place to the seven epiphanies I've embraced at various moments in my professional life that have shaped my thinking about helping people change for the better. It's a recent development. I couldn't have imagined it five or ten years ago. I wasn't ready.

To understand the Life Plan Review concept in the next chapter, it helps to be conversant with the epiphanies that have made such a profound impression on me, how they came to be combined, and why the sum of their parts matters.

1. REFERENT GROUP

Let's return to something we discussed in chapter 2. In the mid-1970s, when Roosevelt Thomas, Jr., introduced me to his idea of referent groups, I had a narrow appreciation of its significance, seeing it as a concept he devised to educate corporate America about the need for diversity in the workplace. Roosevelt believed that an organization was richer and stronger when it included a wide range of differences. The referent group concept was the structure he created to help people understand that if an individual identified with a particular referent group, his or her desire for approval from this group shaped his or her behavior and performance. People would do almost anything to be accepted by the tribe they identify with. Part of his structure for corporate America was a distinction between what he called *preference* and *requirement*. A person's preferences—how they dress, the music they like, the political views they hold—are not relevant if the same person meets or exceeds the requirements of the job. If leaders could accept that distinction—that a direct report's preferences don't have to correlate with the job's requirements—it would allow a lot of differences and eccentricities in the workplace. Leaders would be less aggrieved by superficialities, less obsessed with conformity, and their direct reports would feel more welcome. It was a brilliant insight, aimed at enlightening a leader's point of view about individuals on a team.

I saw the concept from the viewpoint of how it helped executives become better leaders. I failed to appreciate the power of referent groups from the other side, namely, the viewpoint of the referent group members. I also wasn't very adept at applying the concept beyond the workplace, or, for that matter, in my own life. For decades I'd been frustrated by otherwise intelligent people whose social values and knowledge base didn't make sense to me. How could they believe things that, at least to me, were so ignorant and illogical? My confusion persisted well into my sixties. Then I recalled Roosevelt Thomas's main point: If you know a person's referent group—to whom or what they feel deeply connected, whom they want to impress, whose respect they crave—you can understand why they talk and think and behave the way they do. You don't have to agree with them, but you are less likely to dismiss them as brainwashed or uninformed. At the same time, you realize that your views may appear equally incomprehensible to them. It made me more tolerant, almost empathic. It also started me thinking about the utility of referent groups. Was there a structure into which I could fold Roosevelt's insight to help people change their behavior?

Roosevelt Thomas was a giant onto whose shoulders I should have climbed much sooner.

2. FEEDFORWARD

"Feedforward" is a word I started using after a conversation with John Katzenbach when I began coaching CEOs. It was my counterpoint to "feedback," the more common term for an exchange of workplace opinion. Whereas feedback comprises people's opinion of your past behavior, feedforward represents other people's ideas that you should be using in the future. Feedforward was the final structural element in a client's twelve-to-eighteen-month campaign of changing one agreed-upon behavior—after the client commits to the change, publicly announces the intention to change, apologizes for past poor behavior, and asks people to point out any backsliding, always thanking them for the help. The feedforward step was not complicated:

- After you pick the one behavior you intend to change, make your intention known in a one-on-one conversation with someone you know.

- Ask that person—it could be anyone, not necessarily a co-worker—for two suggestions that might help you achieve your goal.
- Listen without judgment, then say "Thank you."
- Do not promise to act upon every idea. Just accept it and promise to do what you can.
- Repeat these steps with your other stakeholders.

Feedforward was an instant hit with the CEOs, unaccustomed as they were to receiving candid advice from their subordinates. It brought discussions about their behavior down to the intimate scale of two human beings talking. It worked because, while successful people don't necessarily enjoy criticism, they welcome ideas for the future. Plus, the CEOs didn't have to act on any of the suggestions. They were only required to listen, then say "Thank you."

At some point, I suggested that the CEOs return the favor and ask their counterparts to identify something they would like to change, turning the conversation into a two-way exchange. The advice givers were rarely members of the CEOs senior management team; they were farther down the food chain. Yet feedforward allowed them to talk as equals with the boss—just two people helping each other. (Think Barack Obama playing basketball with the White House staff during his presidency. On the court, rank doesn't matter; everyone—the president and his teammates and opponents—is equal.)

Feedforward is a very easy and welcome concept to grasp (because it's an insight or tip, not a critique), even when it's being exchanged between strangers. I was one of the speakers at a big event in Moscow, in an arena of fifty thousand people, most listening to me in translation. I asked the crowd to stand up. Find a partner. Introduce yourself. Pick one thing to improve. Ask for feedforward. Say thank you. Ask your partner what he or she would like to improve, then offer feedforward. Keep repeating with new partners until I say stop. The volume and temperature in the hall was palpably higher as I stood onstage for ten minutes and watched fifty thousand people animatedly talking to one another.

The structure of feedforward created something I didn't see every day in the upper reaches of a corporate hierarchy: *reciprocity with genuine goodwill and no judgment.*

3. STAKEHOLDER-CENTERED COACHING

I picked up this next idea from Peter Drucker's well-known interrogatory, "Who is your customer and what does your customer value?" I turned it into stakeholder-centered coaching. Among Drucker's many insights, I contend, his tight focus on the customer will be his most lasting. Drucker believed that everything in business begins with the customer. When he asked "Who is your customer?" he was guiding us to adopt his expansive definition of "customer." A customer is much more than someone who pays for your product or service. A customer could be someone you never meet, such as the end consumer of your product or service, or the decision maker who approves the buy, or a private citizen engaged in refining and repurposing your product for his own purposes, or a public figure who can influence other future customers. Drucker was making the point that, since so many situations in our lives are not so nakedly transactional as the you-buy-what-I-sell exchange between vendor and customer—especially when money isn't changing hands—identifying the "customer" in every circumstance can be a complex challenge. It's not necessarily who you think it is.

This was an insight that hit me hard. It eventually struck me in my coaching practice that my clients also had to broaden their definition of who their customer was—and in the primary position, above all others, were all the people who worked for my client. After all, the leader's co-workers benefited personally and professionally if the leader improved his or her behavior. So I tweaked Drucker's "customer" into "stakeholder"—to emphasize to clients that their employees had a personal investment, or stake, in their improvement. I wanted my CEO clients to think of themselves as servant-leaders, always placing top priority on doing what their employees—that is, their stakeholders—valued before worrying about themselves. The structure I provided was stakeholder-centric, not leader-centric. It was transactional too, a win-win. Leaders earned their employees' respect. Employees earned their CEOs' gratitude.*

It was a fresh perspective that had value beyond the workplace. People in customer-facing enterprises do not survive if they're rude and thoughtless with customers. They display their best behavior to the customer, often better than they do with their co-workers and family. In my experience, when leaders become inured to stakeholder-centered thinking at work, that thoughtfulness eventually seeps into their personal life as well. They're nicer to the people they love—their stakeholders at home. Everyone in their life has become a "customer." When that happens, you are creating an environment around you that is more forgiving, helpful, and kind. People will flock to such a place—and stay there.

---

* On August 19, 2019, the Business Roundtable in a statement signed by 181 CEOs formally endorsed the concept of benefitting all major stakeholders as the purpose of the corporation.

4. BPR

BPR stands for Business Plan Review. Recall former Ford CEO Alan Mulally's way of structuring a weekly meeting in an organization. I've already discussed it in chapter 4. Alan explained this brilliant leadership concept to me when we started working together but I wasn't paying full attention. I thought it was a rigid schematic for running a meeting—fixed time and day, mandatory attendance, five minutes to report progress, traffic light colors (red, yellow, green) to grade status updates, no judgment, no cynicism, and other rules—the kind of structure that would fascinate a superior engineer like Alan. He took the concept with him to Ford and made it the managerial centerpiece of his transformation of the failing automaker. On closer inspection, I saw that the BPR wasn't cold and bloodlessly technocratic; it was grounded in a piercing understanding of people, as if Alan had internalized Drucker's ideas about the "customer" and employed the weekly BPR to treat his executive team not as his direct reports but rather as stakeholders in one another's success, with each executive representing additional groups of stakeholders (customers, suppliers, members of the community, etc.). In doing so, it made everyone in the BPR accountable to both themselves and the group, meeting their dual need for internal validation and belonging to something greater than themselves.

With the BPR, Alan the engineer had built an impregnable fortress that was adaptable to any enterprise and goal. If only I could figure out how to apply it to helping successful people achieve positive lasting change in their behavior.

5. THE "WHAT'S NEXT" WEEKEND

Around 2005 I started inviting a handful of clients to my home for two-day "What's Next?" sessions to help them figure out the next phase of their lives. I'd kept in touch with most of my clients long after our one-on-one work was finished, all the way up to the inescapable day when they had to groom a successor and consider moving on. (My advice was always the same: *Better to stay a year too short than a minute too long.* In other words, leave now, at the top. Never wait for the board to ask you to go. The candidates in line to succeed you won't resent you for it.) Even after they departed, I continued to be involved in helping them decide what to do next. I already knew that successful leaders have many next-step options—consulting, teaching, private equity, philanthropy, boards of directors, another CEO position, skiing in Aspen—but a full menu of options doesn't make choosing easier. When you can do anything and no longer need the paycheck, it's easy to stall in place, doing nothing. One client referred to it as "third-act trouble." The descent from the summit is always more dangerous than the climb.

The more interesting revelation after a few installments of the "What's Next?" weekend was how isolated many of the participants felt, and how eager they were to talk, especially the former CEOs. The top of the ladder is a lonely place; few of them had peers to whom they could talk candidly. The "What's Next?" weekends provided them with a venue to talk with people they respected about anything and everything, revealing that all of us have similar problems and in the right environment—a small group session gathering people of varied backgrounds but similar situations—we are willing to open up and share them. These weekends became the highlight of each year.

6. DAILY QUESTIONS

We are superior planners and inferior doers. Daily Questions is the tool I picked up a decade and a half ago to deal with my repeating pattern of well-meaning intention followed by unreliable execution. I explained it in detail in *Triggers,* including a list of the twenty-two questions that test my daily resolve to match execution with intention, doing with planning. The key: Each question begins with "Did I do my best to . . ." followed by a specific goal such as "Set clear goals?" and "Exercise?" and "Not waste energy on what you cannot change?" At day's end I score each question from a low of 1 to a high of 10, based on how well I tried. The process measures effort, not results. We can't always control the outcome, but all of us can try. Because I need help sticking to the plan, some years ago I hired a "coach" to call me each evening for my scores. It's the best enforcement routine I've come across for earning a desired outcome. But it can be painful; it's disheartening to regularly post 1's and 2's for goals that you claim really matter to you. The pain eventually leads to giving up. But if you stay with it, it works. For anything.

I didn't invent this. Credit goes to Ben Franklin, America's founding father of self-improvement ("A penny saved is a penny earned").

In addition to including a daily to-do list in his *Autobiography* ("Rise, wash, and address the *Powerful Goodness;* contrive day's business and take the resolution of the day; prosecute the present study; and breakfast"), Franklin also described a longer-term self-monitoring regimen. He listed thirteen virtues that he wanted

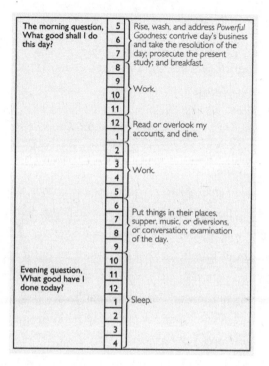

The morning question, What good shall I do this day?	5	Rise, wash, and address *Powerful Goodness*; contrive day's business and take the resolution of the day; prosecute the present study; and breakfast.
	6	
	7	
	8	
	9	Work.
	10	
	11	
	12	Read or overlook my accounts, and dine.
	1	
	2	
	3	Work.
	4	
	5	
	6	Put things in their places, supper, music, or diversions, or conversation; examination of the day.
	7	
	8	
	9	
	10	
Evening question, What good have I done today?	11	
	12	
	1	Sleep.
	2	
	3	
	4	

to perfect within himself.* Rather than tackle all thirteen at once (the quintessential unrealistic goal), Franklin chose one value at a time and fixed on it until he mastered it. Every time he faltered, he marked it down in a book, then added up the blemishes at day's end. When the total came to zero, he declared victory and moved on to the next virtue. Although the routine is more than 250 years old, it's still very contemporary. (It reminds me of NBA sharpshooter Steph Curry's Rule of 100 shooting drill: Curry practices jump shots from five spots on the court, not moving on to the next

---

*Temperance, Silence, Order, Resolution, Frugality, Industry, Sincerity, Justice, Moderation, Cleanliness, Chastity, Tranquility, Humility.

spot until he sinks twenty shots in a row. One miss and he restarts at zero.) It's the inspirational foundation for Daily Questions.

7. 100 COACHES

Placing yourself in a community is the most recent structural element I've taken to heart—and also the one that unlocked the earning puzzle for me.

When Ayse Birsel asked me to name my heroes, she made me aspire to something I could not have anticipated. Saying out loud that Buddha was my hero got the ball rolling. One of the interesting things about Buddha is that he lived three millennia ago and left no written record of his teachings, and yet an estimated 560 million people in the world practice Buddhism. How did that happen? The answer: Buddha gave away all he knew and the recipients of his gift spread the word.

In my own tiny way, I could do the same. The idea came to me on my daily walk in May 2016. The moment I returned home from the walk, I grabbed my phone and impulsively made a thirty-second video selfie in my backyard offering to teach all I know to fifteen applicants with the sole requirement that each adoptee promise to do the same sometime in the future. I called it my 15 Coaches program. I posted the selfie on Linkedin, expecting a small trickle of responses. A day later I had received two thousand applications, which ultimately reached eighteen thousand. Most of the applicants were strangers. But there were also familiar names: coaches and academic stars; HR executives I'd worked with; entrepreneurs and CEOs; and friends. I enlarged my ambition slightly, selecting twenty-five people. We met for the first time in early 2017 in Boston, where I could explain the coaching process and get to know each of my adoptees better. My plan was to coach each of the twenty-five people the same way I conducted my one-on-one coaching with successful leaders, with lots of check-in calls and making myself available. It was a heavy time commitment. In my busiest years I could handle eight one-on-one clients. Now I was taking on three times the workload. But I was okay with it. In my mind, this was a legacy project in which I regarded my adoptees as twenty-five individual assignments rather than a collective group. If the enterprise was a wheel, I was the hub, they were the spokes. The one thing they had in common was *me*. (Remarkably, my enthusiasm for anything soars when I am the center of attention.)

I didn't anticipate that they might have a better idea. The learning curve on my coaching process is short and my adoptees turned out to be quick studies. After a few months they realized they didn't need me. Rather, they turned to one another to swap stories and ideas and support. My would-be acolytes were becoming their own referent group. They were also eager to bring in new members, a notion I hadn't considered but immediately appreciated (strong communities insist on growing, weak ones refuse to). Within a year, 25 Coaches was 100 Coaches. There was no nominating or interview process (we weren't a country club or honor society). If a member knew someone who might benefit from being in our enclave, that person was in, welcomed as that member's particular adoptee. This made the group incredibly diverse, always a good thing.

I'd made fitful attempts at forming a professional community before, but 100 Coaches was turning into something special. I wasn't sure why until I started hearing that coaches in London, New York, Boston, and other cities were getting together socially throughout the year. When a member from Tel Aviv alerted the group that she'd be visiting San Diego, local members invited me to a dinner party they'd organized for her. It was an eye-opening scene. There was no self-promotion and networking in the room. It was more like a family reunion without any of the crazy uncles and stressful family backstories—a gathering of people in a judgment-free zone celebrating their luck at having met one another.

These seven ideas have one thing in common: They are not meant to be pursued alone. They are most effective when two or more people are involved. In other words, the concepts are more robust in an environment that we call a community. Even the ostensibly solo ritual of Daily Questions works better with a partner checking in nightly for your scores; it elevates your accountability and your potential to stay the course.

I'm neither surprised nor saddened that it took me four decades to connect the dots. I had to earn each idea in my own time—when I was ready to hear it. Alan's BPR and his insights about group dynamics in a weekly meeting were certainly a turning point. One day it hit me that if we could take the relentless self-monitoring of Daily Questions and combine it with the long-term benefits that Alan's Business Plan Review provided, we'd have a structure that could apply to any life. Alan agreed. We called it the Life Plan Review.

In January 2020, 160 members of our expanding 100 Coaches community traveled from all over the world to a three-day conference I hosted in San Diego. As I watched the 100 Coaches members enjoying themselves that weekend, I marveled at the big-hearted community I had unintentionally created. It was nothing short of a miracle.

Six weeks later the world went into a pandemic lockdown—and everything changed. The coronavirus pandemic was a dire threat to people's health, livelihood, and financial security, but it also was

❶ Referent Group
Tribal affinities shape our choices

❷ Feedforward
Flip side of feedback: ideas for future, not critique of past

❸ Stakeholder-Centered Coaching
Who are your "customers" and what do they value?

❹ Business Plan Review
Weekly meeting to report "on-plan" progress, no judgment, no cynicism

BPR

❺ The "What's Next" Weekend
2-day small-group sessions about the next phase of life

❻ Daily Questions
Monitoring effort daily to match execution with intention

❼ 100 Coaches
Creating a community of people helping each other be better, no other agendas

100

an attack on our 100 Coaches community. Catastrophic events test the health of a community. Weak ones collapse. Strong ones step up their game and become even stronger. Which one were we?

Among the presentations to the group in San Diego before the lockdown was my introduction, with Alan Mulally's help, of the Life Plan Review concept. It combined the elements that I valued in helping people achieve meaningful change, not the least of which was the binding power of community. The Life Plan Review is a concept that helped fortify our group in a year like no other. If you take away only one idea from these pages, this is the one.

CHAPTER 10

THE LPR

———————

The objective of the Life Plan Review, or LPR, is to close the gap between what you plan to do in your life and what you actually get done.

Its method is contained in the three words in its name. Life. Plan. Review. It presumes that you've decided what you want your *life* to be and what the future you looks like if everything goes according to *plan*. But unlike so many other goal-oriented self-improvement systems, it doesn't rely on exhortations for you to be more heroic in motivation, habit, resourcefulness, and courage. The LPR is an exercise in self-monitoring: You are asked to conduct a weekly *review* of your effort to earn the life you claim to desire. It measures how hard you try, presuming your lapses rather than your steadfastness, honoring the likelihood that you will fall short of perfection most weeks. How much fallibility, denial, and inertia you are willing to accept in your life and what you will do about it is solely up to you. The LPR asks only that you pay attention to your level of trying. There is no earning without heroic effort. And then, like a trainer demanding one more set of crunches, it has one more ask: You must share your results with other people—in a community—not only to recite numbers but to compare notes and help one another.

The LPR is a simple four-step structure that loses much of its power without a community:

Step 1. In the LPR, you and each member of the weekly meeting take turns reporting your answers to a fixed set of six questions that have been documented to improve your life. "Did I do my best to . . ."

1. Set clear goals?
2. Make progress toward achieving my goals?
3. Find meaning?
4. Be happy?
5. Maintain and build positive relationships?
6. Be fully engaged?

You answer each question by reporting a number on a 1 to 10 scale (10 being the best) that measures your level of effort, not your results. Segregating effort from results is critical because it forces you to acknowledge that you can't always control your results (stuff happens), but you have no excuse for not trying.

Step 2. In the days between the weekly LPR meetings you track these questions daily—to create the habit of self-monitoring. It's a ritual as necessary as eating breakfast or brushing your teeth. I prefer to score myself at the end of each day and report my scores on a ten o'clock call with my coach. But I'm not doctrinaire about *when* you answer the questions. Some people wait until the next morning, preferring to sleep on their answers and use the previous day's high or low scores to motivate them through a new day. The key is to accumulate the data so you can see instructive patterns: Where are you trending poorly and where are you in control?

Feel free to add your own questions to my list, or subtract a question or two that doesn't apply. There's nothing sacred about these six, although they meet much of the Recommended Daily Allowance of nutritional ingredients required to earn your life. Goal setting, goal achievement, meaning, happiness, relationships, and engagement are fairly broad terms, but they are sufficiently roomy to accommodate all of the details, however extraordinary or eccentric, in each of our lives. I could have included other questions, such as:

- Did I do my best to express gratitude?
- Did I do my best to forgive the previous me?
- Did I do my best to add value to someone's life?

These questions used to be on my list. But I've been doing this process for two decades. It's a dynamic process, meaning you're supposed to improve and create new stretch goals. It would be dispiriting if I didn't make progress doing this daily review—and adapt the questions as I changed for the better. Along the way, I realized I didn't need to track these three questions anymore. I'm pretty good at thanking others. I'm world-class at forgiving myself. And when I'm not getting paid to add value to someone's life, I do it pro bono. The six questions that remain are existentially demanding and huge in scope—and I doubt I'll ever get so good at them that I can stop trying.

Step 3. Review your plan for relevance and personal need once a week. When you measure effort, you are monitoring the quality of your trying. But from time to time you should also review the purpose of your trying. Are you making a meaningful effort to achieve a now meaningless goal?

Trying is a relative value, neither fixed nor objective nor precise.

It's an opinion by the only qualified person to have that opinion— you. And it changes over time in the course of pursuing a goal. For example, if a personal trainer asked the out-of-shape you to bang out twenty push-ups at your first training session, even a mighty 10 for effort might not get you through all twenty push-ups. Six months later, the well-conditioned you would knock out the same twenty push-ups at a relatively effortless 2. The longer you do something, the less effort you need to do it well. But like the frog in slowly heating water, you might not notice how the passage of time lowers the bar on your effort. The temptation is to settle for less effort to stay in place (i.e., keep doing twenty push-ups); the challenge is to increase your effort to reach your goal (i.e., raise your workload to thirty push-ups, then forty, and so on).

Reviewing your effort is one way to reconsider the value of your goals. If you want to keep the goal, maybe it's time to recalibrate your effort upward. If you're no longer willing to make the required effort, maybe it's time for a new goal.

Step 4. Don't do this alone. This advice is inherently solved by the key feature of an LPR meeting: It is a group event. It places you with a community of like-minded souls. Common sense should tell you that reviewing your plan in the select company of others is vastly superior to reviewing your plan alone. Why would you try to adhere to an ambitious life plan and refuse to share the experience with anyone else, especially if you didn't have to? What added value does going solo bring to the endeavor? It would be like baking a birthday cake to eat by yourself or giving a speech to an empty room.

Consider the game of golf. Although it's one of the rare sports activities that can be enjoyably pursued alone—skiing, swimming, cycling, and running also come to mind—it offers the most convincing argument for playing well with others. It's also a note-for-note model for the benefits of the LPR.

An avid golfer will play a round by himself when playing partners are unavailable, or he's pressed for time, or he wants to work on parts of his game. But if he catches up to another solo player on the course, the two singles will immediately form a twosome. It's one of the many endearing examples of golf etiquette: Single players are never left to play alone unless they prefer it.

Given the choice, the same avid golfer would always prefer playing in a foursome, whether the group is filled out with friends, family, or strangers. Golf is the most social of all sports. You walk the course together, chatting between shots about business, vacation, or events of the day. Sometimes you even take a break midway through the round to share a meal.

These sociability elements are why a golf foursome meets all the requirements of a well-run meeting, such as the weekly review of your LPR that I'm recommending. The game embodies the four actions of our earning template, aided and abetted by the connective tissue of community.

It demands *compliance*. In a serious foursome, you show up at the first tee on time, you play the ball as it lies (no improving the situation), you don't get do-overs (aka mulligans), you count every stroke and penalty. There's even a dress code.

It honors *personal accountability*. You own the credit or discredit for every shot. You can't blame your lapses on anyone else. You cannot delude yourself or others about the quality of your game. If you're rusty or unprepared or simply not as good as you claim to be, a round of golf will expose the truth.

It runs on *follow-up* and *measurement*. Players keep score for themselves and their playing partner. You report your score after every hole. You post your score on a public database to maintain an honest handicap index. And no matter how ardently you re-call your good shots and overlook your bad ones in the post-round review with your playing partners, the only admissible evidence is what's written on your scorecard. The game does not tolerate alternative facts.

Most important, the game embodies what I value in a *commu-nity*. There are rules for behavior. Judgment and cynicism are not tolerated. You applaud a player's well-executed shot, say nothing unkind about a poor one. You help search for another player's lost ball.

It's also a community whose members are committed to get-ting better—and sharing their ideas with others. That's not an in-significant distinction. Unlike most one-on-one sports, golf can be a learning experience. If I face off against a professional baseball pitcher or the club tennis pro, the only thing I'll learn is humilia-tion, that I'm not even remotely in their league. Not so in golf. Me-diocre players want to play with better players, knowing that they can elevate their game simply by observing really fine players—the mechanics of their swing, their smooth tempo, the discipline of their pre-shot routine. The better players welcome it; they're very generous with advice if asked (that's feedforward).

It's a gender-blind community, in which anyone can be anyone else's equal or superior in skill and in scoring. In the presence of a good golfer, there's no condescension or interrupting—only respect.

Golf done right venerates meritocracy and justice. Nothing is given. Everything is earned—the result of practice, maximizing talent, and an urge for constant improvement. It embodies our definition of an earned life because the choices, risks, and efforts we make can be directly linked to an experience we value, regardless of our score.

If you replace the word *golf* with *LPR meeting* in the previous paragraphs, you have all the reasons to adopt the LPR and make it a group exercise. Do not be deterred because forming an LPR group seems daunting to you—a logistical headache, too much trouble, more risk than reward. Trust me, it's not. It's a weekly gathering that can save your day, your year, your world. I know, because it saved mine.

ON MARCH 5, 2020, Lyda and I began the process of selling our home of thirty-two years in the San Diego suburbs and moved into a one-bedroom rental ten miles away in La Jolla overlooking the Pacific Ocean. It was a major but not unexpected lifestyle change for us. The immediate plan was to look for a home in Nashville so we could see our five-year-old twin grandkids grow up. We figured we'd camp out in our new one-bedroom rental for a few weeks as we made trips to Nashville, found a place near our daughter Kelly and her children, filled the new home with the furniture we'd placed in storage, and settled down to enjoy our grandparenting years. Professionally, the move wasn't a disruption, just a change of venue. I was still booked out two years into the future with classes and speaking dates, the majority of them overseas. I was more committed than ever to the 100 Coaches community. I had a book to write.

Six days later all our plans went *poof!* Like many Americans, I can pinpoint the moment: Wednesday evening, March 11, when I heard that the NBA had suspended the remainder of its 2020 season, including the playoffs and finals, because of the emerging coronavirus pandemic. For some reason, the sudden disappearance of a major professional sport from the national calendar was the tipping point when American leaders and citizens realized, "This is serious." A week later, California was in lockdown, air travel ceased, my speaking dates were canceled, and I stared out the window at the Pacific Ocean. Lyda and I would be okay. She lives in the present even more comfortably than I do. We didn't look back and kick ourselves for vacating our much larger home a week too soon. Life was still good, plus we had an ocean view.

I was more concerned about the 100 Coaches community. A mere six weeks earlier, Alan Mulally and I had spent four hours teaching the LPR concept to 160 members of our 100 Coaches group at the Hyatt Regency near La Jolla. The first COVID-19 case in California would be confirmed a few days later. But we were oblivious. The future was wide open. Now I worried. If my speaking business could vanish in an instant, what about the younger, less established coaches and teachers and consultants in our community who didn't have the same cushion as the rest of us? They must be in agony. The academics and C-suite executives in 100 Coaches could fend for themselves. But what about the group's many entrepreneurs, like the restaurateur David Chang, my coaching client and dear friend, whose Momofuku empire would surely be imperiled by a viral pandemic? If we were bees, I thought, we would be in the early but rapidly worsening stage of colony collapse.

I felt as if Buddha was testing me, saying, "Okay, dude. You wanted a legacy project? This is your family now. You're going to have to earn your legacy every day by protecting it."

For the first time in my adult life, I had time on my hands, no flight to catch, no meeting to attend, no crowded days on my schedule. Lyda and I were locked down, trying to stay safe. All I had was a sense of responsibility to 100 Coaches and a renewed sense of purpose to protect it.

So I opened up a Zoom account, commandeered a corner of the tiny apartment as my "studio," and announced that I would be hosting a loosely structured seminar every Monday at ten o'clock EST. Everyone was invited. I'd open with a twenty-minute talk on a single subject, then members would break out into groups of three or four to discuss a question or two I posed to them before returning to the entire group to report what they learned. The number of people on the call started growing from thirty-five at the start to more than a hundred on occasion. It was a very diverse international group, from every continent except Antarctica (note to self: need to work on South Pole membership drive). Many were calling in from middle-of-the-night time zones. Some weeks opened with our version of a CNN Breaking News report, for example, Omran Matar, the lawyer turned Eastern Bloc consultant from Belarus, updating us in real time on the revolution happening in the streets of Minsk just outside his window. There was value simply in seeing faces and hearing voices from a global community. Eventually I learned that Zoom has a chat feature and that while I was sermonizing, a lot of people were messaging one another, like high schoolers passing notes in class, setting up calls among themselves later on. I thought I was protecting the community, but the real work was being done by the members at a more granular level. They were saving one another.

By June 2020, it was clear that the pandemic wasn't fading and that Lyda and I wouldn't be moving to Nashville for a year or longer. With everyone stuck at home, the 100 Coaches community offered the perfect opportunity to beta test the LPR (which we'd introduced to them five months earlier just before the lockdown) in a group setting. I conscripted fifty members to commit to answering the six basic LPR questions and reporting their scores on a Zoom call every Saturday or Sunday morning for ten weeks. I repeated my standard warning about effort-based self-monitoring: "It's easy to understand. Very hard to stick with."

When successful people are challenged to grade themselves on effort and then must face their inadequacy in the simple act of trying to achieve a goal they chose, they often give up after two or three weeks. Mostly, though, they feel shame that they failed a test they had written. I expected ten quitters in our fifty-person group, a 20 percent dropout rate.

My coaching partner Mark Thompson and I hosted six one-hour back-to-back calls for eight people each weekend that summer. Attendance was a soft mandatory, but that turned out to be a nonissue. No one skipped out. Not once. Members of the group could choose a 9:00 A.M., 10:30 A.M., or noon time slot on either Saturday or Sunday. Some stuck to the same slot, others switched around—which added a nonscientific wrinkle to my informal study. People weren't accountable to the same group of people each week. On the other hand, there was surely some heightened enthusiasm for the process because people didn't know who they'd be seeing on the call each week. My job was to ensure that everyone got to meet every other individual at least once.

Ten weeks is not long enough to establish lasting positive change in complex targets like engagement and finding meaning and repairing relationships. That's too big an ask in such a short time, nor is it congruent with the LPR's purpose. It's supposed to last a lifetime. But ten weeks is long enough to provide some strong indicators of its value.

Everyone charted their weekly scores, so progress or regression was easy to gauge. Over ten weeks, the members' effort scores increased steadily. By the tenth week, people who had started out below 5 for effort were regularly placing themselves in the 8 to 10 range. My takeaway is that if you can get through the early weeks without giving up, some level of success is inevitable. Reviewing the scores each week in public adds accountability, to the group and to yourself. When you see you're making steady gains, you're less likely to accept regression to the lower depths again.

This is the primary benefit of the LPR. In a matter of weeks you'll notice how brutally it forces you to confront the tough question, "What did I actually do this week to make progress on my goals?" Given our tendencies for superior planning but inferior doing, this is a question we prefer to avoid. The LPR removes that option. This is why participants' scores start improving so quickly. The alternative—reporting poor scores for trying week after week—is too painful to deal with.

WE MADE THE LPR's structure as simple as possible, because simple self-monitoring structures are easier to follow and are therefore less likely to be abandoned midstream. You rate your effort on six or more goals of your choosing every day, then report your scoring average on each question in a weekly group setting. How hard can that be?

Pre-2020 I would have said that the sociability requirement—that people who don't work together have to meet in person at the same time every week—represented the most challenging feature of the LPR. How do you get busy people to show up each week? But the COVID pandemic and the saving graces of videoconferencing apps such as Zoom have taken care of that problem. We've all grown accustomed to seeing one another's faces on screens rather than in person.

Still, as any successful leader knows, the fate of any team begins and ends with personnel selection. How do you cast the characters in your LPR group for maximum appeal so that members want to come back each week? Zoom alone doesn't solve that eternal riddle. You need a strategy to create a group that shows up each week and loves it.

Aim for maximum diversity. This was my big takeaway from the success of my annual What's Next sessions. Start with an equitable gender split, always a must-have. Then mix and match people according to age, culture, nationality, professional rank, and line of work. Do not presume that radically different people might not mix well or be interested in one another. Successful people are innately curious. Diversity should be highlighted, not modulated. That's the point of diversity: The greater the differences among people in a meeting, the fresher and more surprising the viewpoints being shared. When I chose the fifty people for the first ten-week LPR experiment, I modeled myself on Noah filling his ark, with two of each species at most. A typical session had Jan Carlson, the CEO of Europe's largest manufacturer of seat belts and other auto-safety systems, calling in from Stockholm; Gail Miller, a grandmother leading a sprawling family business in Utah; Nankhonde van den Broek, a thirty-nine-year-old nonprofit professional in Zambia taking over her late father's business; Pau Gasol, the thirty-nine-year-old NBA star at the end of his career; Dr. Jim Downing, a surgeon running St. Jude Children's Research Hospital in Memphis; Margo Georgiadis, the CEO of Ancestry in Boston, who was in the process of working herself out of the job by selling Ancestry to a private equity group; and Marguerite Mariscal, the thirty-one-year-old CEO helping Dave Chang reorganize his restaurant empire. You might not seat these seven people at the same wedding table, but in a weekly group meeting where everyone shared the same self-improvement objectives, the chemistry was palpable. Diversity does that.

Group size is more a function of bringing in the right people and leaving out the wrong people. If you have any doubt that a possible choice will add value to the group, don't ignore your concerns simply to fill out the group to achieve your idea of a proper head count. Better to leave out a candidate than to allow him or her to kill the group's vibe. I'd recommend a group of no fewer than five people, no more than eight. And don't let the meeting run longer than ninety minutes.

The LPR is not therapy. It's a gathering of successful people with shared goals for the future, not a gripe session for unsuccessful people with problems. And by "successful" I don't mean people measured solely by their impressive status, power, and paycheck. You're looking for people of any and every stripe who share the same optimism about getting better. They are not victims or martyrs. Do that and you'll always have a roomful of equals where no one is too intimidated to speak up or too self-satisfied to listen.

Someone has to lead the group. If the LPR group was your idea, then you're responsible for running the meeting, preferably with a light touch rather than a heavy fist. Otherwise, your LPR can become, as a fellow coach put it, "overstructured and underfacilitated." In the same way that Alan Mulally was always the facilitator of his BPR meetings at Boeing and Ford (because it was his idea), Mark Thompson and I were the facilitators in our LPRs. It's more an administrative task—calling on people, moving things along, enforcing the "no judgment" rule, maintaining the safe space environment—than a coaching role. Until the group learns to be self-governing, assume that everyone is looking to you to keep the train running on time.

ALONG THE WAY, you'll also notice other benefits to the LPR:

1. YOU CAN APPLY IT TO ANY GOAL

When Alan Mulally and his wife, Nicki, were raising their five children in Seattle, he adapted the Business Plan Review he was using with his team at Boeing into a Family Plan Review at home. On Sunday mornings, he and Nicki and the five kids would show up with their calendars and review what each needed to do and the support they required to get through the week. It was how Alan balanced the five areas in his life—professional, personal, family, spiritual, and recreational—that mattered to him. He'd review his calendar daily, always checking to make sure he was doing what he wanted to do and making a positive difference in one of those five areas. If he saw things getting out of balance, he'd make a midcourse correction and change his calendar. It was also how the family never lost touch with one another.

The LPR need not be restricted only to achieving an earned life in the grandest sense. You can apply it to any way station on the road to the earned life—to any goal, big or small. For example, let's say you decide you want to do something about the environment instead of talking about it all the time. What's stopping you from finding a half dozen environmentally like-minded people, establishing personal goals, and reviewing them each week in a group setting? You're adapting the LPR process into an EPR, your very own Environmental Plan Review. The objective may be narrower and more focused, but the challenge is no less severe. Each week you and the other members have to square off against the bare-knuckled question, "What did I do this week to help save the planet?" In effect, you're determining if you've earned the week or lost it.

The application of the LPR process to any professional or personal challenge is limited only by your imagination and your resourcefulness in recruiting people to join you.

2. THE SAFE SPACE ALSO KEEPS US SAFE FROM OURSELVES

Participants instantly welcome and comply with the no-cynicism, no-judgment atmosphere of an LPR meeting, with one exception: when they talk about themselves. Somehow group members think they're exempt from the LPR's safe space rules if their negativity is not directed at others. Of the sixty sessions I led in our first LPR "season," I can't recall one in which I didn't have to interrupt one or two participants in the middle of a harsh self-indicting judgment of their past behavior. Usually it's a casual confession about a supposed deficiency ("I'm not good at . . ."). I'd urgently wave my arms, saying "Stop, stop, stop!" Then I'd make them raise their hand, say their name, and repeat after me: "Although I've been bad at X in the past, that was a previous me. I do not have an incurable genetic defect that prevents me from changing for the better." They usually get the message the first time they're busted: A safe space is for everyone, including the people we have been.

3. MEASURING EFFORT PUSHES YOU TO DEFINE WHAT MATTERS

When Garry Ridge, the longtime CEO of WD-40 (yes, the blue and yellow can with the red top that's in everyone's home) reported his weekly scores in our LPR group, he always stalled on "Did I do my best to find meaning?" For six consecutive weeks, he'd write down a neutral 5, explaining that he was struggling to define his criteria for "meaning." It's important to know this fact about Garry: He went back to school and earned a master's degree in leadership *after* he became CEO of WD-40, which is like an actor enrolling in acting classes after winning an Academy Award. He is a seeker who takes the practice of management seriously, and he's constantly learning. The LPR played directly into this side of Garry Ridge. He was determined to nail down his definition of "finding meaning." After six weeks of hearing group members describe their criteria for meaning and scratching to find his own definition, Garry showed up with the answer on week 7: "I find meaning," he said, "when the result of what I'm doing matters to me and helps others." Perhaps not an earth-shattering insight to you, but it was to Garry.

This wasn't an isolated incident. When Theresa Park, a New York literary agent turned film producer, told the group that happiness to her wasn't necessarily "a feeling of giddiness," I could see everyone nodding, treating it is an epiphany that immediately redefined happiness for them. Likewise, when Nankhonde van den Broek, calling from Zambia, talked about her primary goal as a new leader of an organization: "I want to observe the tornado without contributing to it," she said. The managers in the group applauded that insight, as if they could put it to immediate use.

This is what happens in the LPR: Insights and clarity sneak up on you, because (a) every day you have to measure your effort on dealing with meaningful issues,* and (b) at week's end you're exposed to smart people discussing those issues. All you have to do is show up and catch the nuggets as they fall from everyone's lips.

4. MAKE THE RIGID STRUCTURE WORK FOR YOU

The rules of an LPR are few, but they are strict—show up every week, be nice, report your scores. But even with the most rigid structures, you can always find room to improvise within the lines. After a few weeks of sessions, I introduced two questions for each participant to wrap up the meeting: *What did you learn this week?* and *What are you proud of this week?* I wasn't trying to provoke anyone; I was just curious. It became a permanent feature of our sessions.

Another time, when I saw a new member visibly in emotional pain (2020 was a rough year for many people), I called an audible. I asked each member to give the newbie one piece of advice that would help him (feedforward). The session went thirty minutes longer than usual, but I believe he was profoundly touched by everyone's concern and generosity. The following week, he was a changed man.

The most valuable feature of the LPR is that people are there

---

* I owe this insight about the value of measuring effort rather than results to my daughter Kelly Goldsmith, who taught me the difference between asking "active" and "passive" questions. "Do you have clear goals?" is passive. "Did you do your best to set clear goals?" is active, because it places the burden on you rather than your situation.

to help one another. If you spot an opportunity during the meeting to make someone's life a little better, seize it. Improvise. Fool around with the format. Call your audible. (And let me know about it. You'll be helping me too.)

5. WHAT HAPPENS AFTER THE LPR CAN BE MORE MEANINGFUL THAN WHAT HAPPENS DURING THE LPR

I learned this from my Monday Zoom groups when I discovered that so many members were connecting afterward and helping one another. I saw this phenomenon repeated with the LPRs. It shouldn't have surprised me, given the confessional nature of the comments in an LPR. After all, people are being asked to talk about their goals and happiness and relationships. They're not giving a progress report on unit sales of moisturizer in the Dallas–Fort Worth metroplex. Emotional honesty invites reciprocal honesty. It motivates people to help one another. And so they connect.

ONE OF THE side pleasures of introducing the LPR to people is how smoothly it incorporates the seven epiphanic concepts that have shaped my coaching career. People who stick with the LPR week after week are essentially their own *referent group*, holding the same beliefs about getting better and benefiting one another. They make maximum use of *feedforward*, i.e., both asking for it and offering it without judgment, only with gratitude. It's *stakeholder-centered* in that the governing mindset of the sessions is that everyone is a stakeholder in everyone else's progress. In structure (a reporting session of progress or regression), meeting cadence (weekly), and attitude (we're gathered to learn and help), it's a spin-off of my friend Alan Mulally's *Business Plan Review*. In the diversity of its members and their naked honesty with one another, it's a copy of my annual *What's Next sessions* with clients. It uses my *Daily Questions* self-monitoring process. Finally, it harnesses the power of community that I came to appreciate with the formation of our *100 Coaches community*.

After season 1 of our LPR experiment ended, the week before Labor Day, I started getting calls and texts from members wondering when I was starting season 2. They missed the weekly get-togethers, which is not something I hear that often. Busy people rarely complain that they don't go to enough meetings. And yet here they were, suffering LPR withdrawal. I regarded it as proof of concept. It told me that the LPR is a structure that addresses something beyond a mere goal such as getting better at X or, for that matter, being a better person or boss or partner. It could address our most basic aspirations and help us find fulfillment—and do it on a continuing basis, as if the process of trying to live an earned life was a virtue worthy of becoming their new habit. The pleas for a season 2 were evidence that the LPR was working better than I imagined. It not only gave people more agency over their progress in life—a heightened sense that it was being earned rather than handed to them—but they were coming back for more. They did not want to leave a community where everyone else was aspiring just like them.

When I say the LPR saved my world, this is what I'm talking about. It brought to mind Lao Tzu's insight about leadership: "A leader is best when people barely know he exists; when his work is done, his aim fulfilled, they will say, 'We did it ourselves.'" In a perilous and challenging year, I set out to protect the 100 Coaches community, and the community ended up protecting itself.

CHAPTER 11

THE LOST ART OF ASKING FOR HELP

A t its core, the LPR is an accountability mechanism. It makes us more accountable for our behavior by making us answerable on a regular basis to other people. It reminds us to measure what's important in our lives and, as a result, attacks one of our most persistent human frailties—our failure each day to actually do what we claim we want to do. That benefit alone makes the LPR a valuable aid for achieving an earned life. The more capable we are at bridging the gap between our Actions, Ambitions, and Aspirations, the more our progress feels validated and, therefore, earned.

Among Peter Drucker's many uncanny management predictions is this: "The leader of the past knew how to tell; the leader of the future will know how to ask." I quickly realized the LPR offered a less obvious but equally valuable benefit to us. Simply by choosing to participate in the LPR process we are overcoming one of the biggest obstacles to living an earned life: *We are asking for help.*

The myth of the self-made individual is one of the more sacred fictions of modern life. It endures because it promises us a just and happy reward that is equal to our persistence, resourcefulness, and hard work. Like most irresistible promises, it deserves our skepticism.

It's not impossible to achieve success on your own to the point where it could be accurately described as self-made. The more salient question is: Why would you want to when you could surely achieve a better result by enlisting people's help along the way? An earned life is not more "earned" or glorious or gratifying—or even more likely—because you tried to achieve it all by yourself.

Too many of us try to go it alone. Our near-clinical reluctance to ask for help is not a genetic defect, like color blindness or tone deafness. It is an acquired defect, a behavioral failing we are conditioned to accept from an early age. I didn't learn how companies slyly discourage asking for help in my organizational psychology classes in grad school. I had to learn it on the job.

In 1979, I was working at IBM headquarters in Armonk, New York, at a time when IBM was the most admired company in the world, the gold standard in management. IBM had a problem: Its managers were not perceived internally as doing a good job coaching their direct reports. I was called in to review IBM's program in which they trained managers to be good coaches. Over the years they had spent millions of dollars on the program—with negligible improvement to show for it. Managers were still bad at coaching their direct reports. I was invited to Armonk for a firsthand look to figure out what went wrong and why. When I interviewed employees, a typical interview went like this:

I asked the direct reports:

Q: Does your manager do a good job providing coaching?
A: No.

I asked the managers:

Q: Do your direct reports ever ask you for coaching?
A: No, never.

Back to the direct reports.

Q: Do you ask your manager for coaching?
A: No.

Curious about IBM's performance appraisal system, I analyzed the employees' year-end reviews and discovered this is how IBM defined a top performer: *Performs effectively with no need for coaching.* Basically, IBM had created a vicious cycle whereby if the manager offered coaching, the employee was incentivized to respond, "No, thank you, boss. I perform effectively with no need for coaching." (You can't make this up!)

I'd like to say IBM's dilemma was unique. But it wasn't; they were merely the platinum-plated example of companies making the same mistake. It started at the top rungs of IBM management, few of whom would debase themselves by admitting they needed help. To ask for help was deemed a sign of weakness. You asked for help when (a) you didn't know something, (b) you couldn't do something, or (c) you lacked resources. In other (more pejorative) words, you asked for help because of your:

- ignorance,
- incompetence, or
- neediness

None of these is a good look. Since people in any organization tended to model their behavior on their bosses', the CEO's attitude about seeking help swiftly flowed down the hierarchy and settled in place for everyone to emulate. Sure, corporations actively hired trainers to teach classes on generalized topics that we had learned in business school—teamwork, situational leadership, decentralization, total quality, Six Sigma, "excellence," and the rest—but these were more like the continuing education courses that doctors and CPAs were required to take to maintain their professional accreditation.

As for one-on-one coaching between managers and staff—which begins when an individual reveals his or her vulnerability and says "I need help"—it was barely on anyone's radar in the corporate environment. Something that resembled coaching took place in highly technical fields—medicine, the performing arts, craft trades like carpentry and plumbing—in which skills were passed on in a traditional master-and-apprentice relationship. But this wasn't coaching; it was just a more intimate, hands-on form of teaching. It was a finite process by which eventually the apprentice learns enough to graduate into expertise. Coaching, on the other hand, is an ongoing process, as open-ended as our desire to continue improving. The difference between teaching and coaching is the difference between "I want to learn" and "I need help to get better and better."

I didn't fully appreciate this distinction during my time in Armonk. As with most consequential advances in my career, clarity began a few months later with someone else's suggestion—in this case, a phone call from the CEO of a major pharmaceutical company.

I had just given a leadership clinic to the human resources department at the CEO's company. He attended the session and must have heard something that struck a nerve. He had an unusual request. He said, "I've got this guy running a big division who delivers his numbers every quarter. He's a young, smart, ethical, motivated, creative, charismatic, arrogant, stubborn, know-it-all jerk. Our company is built on team values, and no one thinks he's a team player. It would be worth a fortune to us if we could turn this guy around. Otherwise, he's out of here."

I had never worked one-on-one with an executive before (the field of executive coaching as we know it today did not exist) and certainly not with someone who was one click away from the CEO's chair at a multi-billion-dollar company. From the CEO's terse description, I had met this fellow many times already. He was the kind of guy who had triumphed at every rung of the achievement ladder. He liked to win, whether it was at work, or playing darts, or arguing with a stranger. He'd had "high potential" stamped on his forehead since day one in the workplace. Would someone whose entire life was an affirmation of always being right accept my help?

I had taught plenty of midlevel managers in groups before. These were people on the verge of success but not quite there yet. Could my methods work on a more elite flight of executive material on a one-on-one basis? Could I take someone who was demonstrably successful and make him or her more successful?

I told the CEO, "I might be able to help."

The CEO sighed. "I doubt it."

"Tell you what," I said. "I'll work with him for a year. If he gets better, pay me. If not, it's all free."

The next day I caught a return flight to New York City to meet the CEO and my first one-on-one coaching client.

I had a big advantage with that first client. He had no choice but to commit to being coached. If he didn't, he'd be out of a job. Fortunately, he had the work ethic and desire to change; he got better and I got paid. But as I picked up more clients like him, I learned to create an environment in which a leader did not feel embarrassed to ask for help. It harked back to the paradox I noticed at IBM: The company's leaders thought coaching was valuable for employees but not for themselves. This was nonsense, of course. None of us is perfect. We're all flawed human beings. We all should be asking for help. My breakthrough was reminding my accomplished clients of this eternal truth.

One of the ways I did this was asking them to list all the things they could do as a leader to support the people they worked with. I called this the Needs Exercise: *What do your people need from you?*

They'd rattle off the obvious stuff: support, recognition, a sense of belonging and purpose. Then they'd go deeper. People needed to be loved, and heard, and respected. They needed to feel loyal to something and receive loyalty back in return. They needed to be fairly rewarded for doing a good job, not overlooked or discounted.

"That's a lot of neediness among your staff members," I'd say to my CEO client. "What about turning it around on yourself? Admit that you need the same things. You're no better than your employees. One or two of them might even become the organization's leaders after you're gone. They are you."

I wanted clients to see that when they trumpeted their roles as supportive leaders and in the same self-contradictory breath asserted that they did not require equal support themselves, they were in fact demeaning their employees and the dignity of their needs. And this didn't go unnoticed by the employees. It was a massive failure in leadership.

Since successful leaders recoil at the thought of failing at anything, it didn't take clients long to overcome their shame and abhorrence for the phrase "I need help"—and accept coaching. They recognized that they would perform better with help, not without it. It's amazing that smart people had to be told this, but those were the times. Nowadays, the widespread demand for executive coaching is evidence that the company values its leaders and is willing to pay for them to get better.

For a lot less money, committing to the LPR provides many of the same coaching benefits. Above all, it gives you permission to say, "I want to get better and I need help." This acknowledgment is the price of admission to the LPR.

The more I conducted the Needs Exercise with clients, the more I noticed that needing anything, whether it was help or respect or time off or a second chance, had somehow evolved into an object of derision in the workplace, a character flaw, a weakness as objectionable as being ignorant or incompetent.

The reviled need that continues to baffle me most is our need for approval. If you Google "need for approval," the first hundred entries describe it as a psychological defect, selectively illustrated by cringeworthy behavior such as valuing the opinions of others more than your own, and agreeing with people even when you actually disagree, and praising people in order to be liked by them. When had seeking approval or recognition become a bad thing, a synonym for phoniness and sycophancy and tactical dissembling? How had seeking approval or recognition been demoted to *neediness?*

In the workplace, I believe our problem with approval, like our problem with asking for help, starts at the top. My experience with successful leaders is that they're sensitive to employees' need for approval and recognition and are very adept at providing it. But for the same reasons they won't admit they need help, they're reluctant to acknowledge their own need for approval or recognition. A leader's internal sense of validation—i.e., self-approval—should be enough, they tell themselves. Anything else is grandstanding, the equivalent of turning on the Applause sign for yourself. Net result: the CEO's attitude filters down the line until approval and recognition are denied their rightful place throughout the organization.

This "Do as I say, not as I do" hesitation to seek approval even infects experts on the subject. My great friend (and 100 Coaches member) Chester Elton is the world's authority on the value of recognition in the workplace. I asked whether he encountered this reluctance to seek recognition among leaders he's worked with.

He said, "I may not be the right person to ask. I went through a period in my life when I was feeling really down. So I wrote a note to a dozen friends saying, 'I talk about recognition all day. To be honest, I can use some recognition myself right now.' I received a dozen wonderful letters that made me feel fantastic. They revived me."

"Sounds like you're the perfect person to ask," I said.

"That was one time, twenty years ago. I never did it again," he said, recognizing his do-as-I-say-not-as-I-do error. "But I should and I will."

FOR MANY YEARS now helping leaders accept and emphasize their needs has been a big part of my coaching. Sometimes it's the only advice they need.

I started coaching Hubert Joly in 2010 when he was CEO of Carlson, the privately owned hospitality giant in Minneapolis. I did my usual setup routine: I interviewed Hubert's direct reports and the Carlson board of directors, distilling their feedback into two reports. First, I sent Hubert the report of all the positive feedback, advising him to appreciate it. The next day I sent the longer report about his negatives, telling him to digest it slowly. Although he was already a respected leader, of the twenty executive bad habits

I'd listed in *What Got You Here Won't Get You There*, Hubert, by his count, was guilty of thirteen. His big issue was thinking he always had to add value, out of which flowed his other issues, such as needing to win too much and passing judgment.

Then we met, and I could see where his reputedly excessive need to be right came from. He'd been at the top of his class at the most elite schools in his native France. He'd been a star consultant at McKinsey. In his thirties, he became president of EDS-France, then moved to the United States, where he eventually rose to the top of Carlson. But I also learned he was a bit of a religious scholar who'd collaborated with two monks from the Congregation of St. John (they'd met at business school) on articles about the nature of work. He was well read not only in the Old and New Testaments but in the Koran and the teachings of Eastern religions too. I liked him immediately.

I didn't belabor each of the bad habits in his report. I told him to pick three that he wanted to work on and commit to improving. Then the coaching process began—the apologizing to colleagues for past behavior, the promising to do better, the asking for help, and the grateful acceptance of feedforward advice.

Two years later, Hubert became CEO of Best Buy, where he faced one of the biggest challenges in American business: saving a big-box electronics retailer competing on price against Amazon. Hubert's improvement before he started at Best Buy was so significant, he could have taken a victory lap and ended our coaching relationship. But he didn't, for two reasons: (1) he was committed to continuous self-improvement, having grown very comfortable with expressing his need for help, and (2) he wanted his new colleagues at Best Buy to see the self-improvement process in practice. So he invited me to come along for the ride as his coach at his new job. He went public with his need for help, in effect telling his staff, "I have a coach. I need feedback. You need feedback too."

His strategy for Best Buy was to compete with online retailers not on price, but rather by offering better "advice, convenience, and service." This meant that when a customer came to one of Best Buy's one-thousand-plus showrooms, the floor people had to be so knowledgeable and enthusiastic that the customer would have no reason to buy anywhere else. In other words, Hubert was betting the store solely on the employees of Best Buy.

As Hubert became more acquainted with Best Buy and we discussed how to get the workforce behind his strategy, he came up with a remarkably counterintuitive strategy. Hubert wasn't going to help the employees in the usual top-down management approach. Quite the opposite. He would ask them to help him. He would expose his vulnerabilities publicly to them, acknowledging his need for help at every step. He would ask for their approval, not in the form of personal "Do you like me?" assurances, but rather in the form of their "buy-in" and commitment to his strategy. Like a great salesperson always asking for the order or a savvy politician never forgetting to ask citizens for their vote, Hubert's ask went deep and close to the bone. He asked employees for their belief in his strategy by asking for their "heart." And they gave it to him. All he had to do was ask.

In the course of transforming Best Buy—during which the stock price quadrupled and Jeff Bezos of Amazon would say in 2018, "The last five years, since Hubert came to Best Buy, have been remarkable"—Hubert transformed himself as a person as well. To his employees he became a human being, imperfect and vulnerable, willing to admit he didn't know everything and there-fore willing to ask for help. He joined Alan Mulally and Frances Hesselbein as one of my three most successful coaching clients—Alan and Frances because they had to change the least (they were already great when we met and became even greater), Hubert be-cause he changed the most.

IF I CAN leave you with only one piece of advice to increase your probability of creating an earned life, it is this: *Ask for help. You need it more than you know.*

You would not hesitate to call a doctor if you were in extreme physical pain, or a plumber if your kitchen sink was clogged, or a lawyer if you were in legal trouble. You know how to ask for help. And yet there are moments in each day when asking for help is clearly the better choice and you decline to do so. Beware two situ-ations in particular.

The first is when you are ashamed to seek help because doing so will expose your ignorance or incompetence. The teaching pro-fessional at a golf club once told me that fewer than 20 percent of the three hundred members at her club had ever taken a lesson from her. They were too embarrassed by their faulty swing to let her help them. "I pay my bills giving lessons to the thirty or forty best golfers at the club," she said. "They only want to shoot better scores. They don't care how they got there or who helped them. Their scorecard doesn't care either."

The second situation begins when you tell yourself, "I should be able to do this on my own." You fall into this trap when the task you're facing is adjacent to knowledge or a skill you think you already possess. You're driving through a familiar neighborhood, so you should be able to reach your destination with no need for directions from your phone's GPS. You've given speeches before, so you don't need a friend's helping ear to fine-tune a wedding toast or your most important sales presentation of the year.

I do not have this problem anymore, which is why "Did I do my best to ask for help?" is no longer on my list of basic Daily Questions. I declared victory in this battle many years ago, when I asked myself what task or challenge in my life could be more profitably and efficiently dealt with alone rather than with solicited help from other people—and couldn't come up with an answer. You should too.

Consider all the times someone—friend, neighbor, colleague, stranger, even foe—has asked you for help. Did you

- refuse them,
- resent them,
- judge them to be stupid,
- question their competence, or
- deride them behind their back for needing help?

If you're like most good people I know, your first impulse was to help. You'd demur only if you lacked the capacity to help—and you'd probably apologize for it, regarding your inability as somehow *your* failure. The one response you wouldn't offer is an instant and outright *no*.

Before you reject the idea of asking others to help you, consider this: If you are willing to help anyone who asks for your help without thinking ill of them, why would you worry that other people won't be as generous and forgiving when you're the one seeking help? The Golden Rule, by definition, works both ways, never more so than when help is on the table.

An even more meaningful question: How have you felt when you have helped others? I think we can agree that's one of the great feelings, right? Why would you deprive others of the same feeling?

EXERCISE

Write Your History of Help

Here is an exercise in recovered memory and humility.

DO THIS: Make a list of your five to ten proudest achievements, particularly the ones where the accomplishment felt well deserved. Now imagine you were invited to receive an award for each achievement and you were expected to give a thank-you speech in front of all your relatives, colleagues, and friends. Whom would you thank? And why?

I suspect you'll find in each case that you did not succeed without help. I'm not talking merely about instances of unexpected luck and serendipity, but rather the gifts of other people's wisdom and influence that helped advance a project or avoid a catastrophic misjudgment. Without this trip down memory lane, I suspect you will always be underestimating how much assistance you have received in your life.

Once you appreciate all the help you've either forgotten or failed to credit in your life, you are finally ready for the alarming payoff of this exercise. You can imagine—and kick yourself with regret—how much more you could have achieved if you had asked for help more often. Now extend your imagination forward: Where do you need help in the future? And who are the first people you would ask to help you?

CHAPTER 12

WHEN EARNING
BECOMES YOUR HABIT

W hen does earning begin? When does it end? When do we take a time out from all our strivings to savor the process and reevaluate, often concluding we need to earn something new?

In the preceding four chapters we've considered the *discipline* required to achieve an earned life, and how it is an acquired skill, the product of our compliance, accountability, follow-up, measurement, and community. We've also examined the simple structural elements of the LPR, or Life Plan Review, as a system to help us *stay on plan.* And we've been reminded that we do much better when we concede our *need for help.*

Discipline. Staying on plan. Asking for help. The next consequential issue is the matter of *timing.* Achieving an earned life is hard work, often all-consuming. But we're all human. Our resources—energy, motivation, concentration—deplete. When should we step on the accelerator and when do we step back to recover and reboot, balancing the urgency to "always be earning" with our need to reflect on what we've accomplished and what remains to be done?

Earning your life is a long game. Check that: It's *the* long game. You need a strategy anchored in both self-awareness and situational awareness to sustain the urgency and avoid burnout—until earning has become your habit.

1. EARN YOUR BEGINNINGS

In the course of a lifetime, you will experience episodes when one phase of your life ends and another begins. Some of them are predictable markers of modern life: graduation; your first "real" job; marriage; your first house; parenthood; divorce; career success; career failure; the loss of a loved one; a lucky break; a big idea. These moments can be exhilarating or confusing to the point of paralysis ("What do I do next?"). They can be opportunities or crises, turning points or setbacks. Gail Sheehy called them "passages" in her 1977 bestseller of the same name. My late friend Bill Bridges called them *transitions*. (Every few years I revisit his 1979 classic on the subject, suitably titled *Transitions*. Highly recommended reading.)

We all experience these intervals between the old and the new. According to Bill Bridges, "The transition process does not depend on there being a replacement reality waiting in the wings. You are in transition automatically when some part of your life ends."

But we make a grave error if we treat a transition as a lull in the action, the quiet before the storm that allows us to take a time out and passively wait for our next phase—our "replacement reality"—to begin. Our transitions are not voids that we aimlessly roam until we find an escape route. They are living organisms, as alive as other fully engaging parts of our lives.

The American choreographer Twyla Tharp is an expert on transitions, having created more than 160 ballets and modern dances in her fifty-year career. That's 160-plus transition periods between one finished dance and the next new dance. It's also 160-plus temptations—at least three a year—to lie down and take a nap before starting the next piece. Tharp doesn't take the bait. She doesn't wait for the next inspiration to whack her on the side of her head. She proactively seeks it. In her words, she has to "earn her next beginning"—putting the old piece behind her, researching composers, listening to music, working out steps alone for hours with a video camera running so no idea is lost. Then when all of these disconnected parts align, she's ready to start creating. This is how she earns her next beginning. To the untrained eye, what might look like a dead zone of inaction between projects is actually as focused and drenched in sweat as the intense hours rehearsing her dancers before opening night. Transitions to Tharp are not a respite from the earning process; they are one more critical part of it, as hard-earned as anything else she does.

I think Tharp is right about this: Each of us has a unique set of criteria for defining the turning points in our lives, that moment when we begin to disengage with our previous self and start to accommodate the new person we want to become. Whereas a creative artist like Twyla Tharp might identify her transitional moments in a micro sense as the intervals between individual dances, or in a macro sense as the sharp breaks between major stylistic periods in her career (akin to the gap between, say, Picasso's Blue Period and Rose Period), you and I might opt for different markers.

For example, *people* are my markers for the big turning points in my life—specifically, *people who offered me some variation of the You Can Be More speech.* My earliest memory of such a person is Mr. Newton in eleventh grade, who told me a D in math was inexcusable. He expected more from me. This has happened a dozen times in my life. Each of these dozen people, whether they intended it or not, induced a sudden dissatisfaction with my current self and a strong desire to become someone new. I didn't yet know who that person might be, but they nudged me into a transition where I could sort out my options, discover the answer, and earn my next beginning.

The markers you use to interpret the arc of your life are a deeply personal choice. One executive told me his major inflection points are his screw-ups—because he turned the shame-filled memory of each fiasco into a teachable moment, a mistake never to be repeated. Another said it was in the half dozen moments when he realized he was no longer the most junior person in the room and that his influence had grown. He marked the passage of time by each moment he was made aware of his rising professional stature. An industrial designer marks off the inflection points in her career through the products she designed. Each design is like a milestone marking off the distance she has traveled between one product and the next. When she looks at the designs in chronological order, she sees the evidence of the evolving person she was when she brought each product to market.

Age is also a factor. Your perspective on your major turning points changes with the accumulated years. In 2022, I can interpret my life through the lens of a dozen people's influence on me over a span of seventy-three years, whereas an eighteen-year-old's unit of measurement might be the thirteen grades between kindergarten and senior year of high school, with summer break as the transition from one phase to the next. Later in life, the youthful transitions that felt like turning points will fade into the background, while other moments, unappreciated at the time, will emerge as defining ones. When she's seventy-three like me, I doubt if she'll include more than one high school episode among her turning points.

You cannot know if you've begun to earn your next beginning until you know you're in transition. You cannot appreciate your transitions until you have a method for marking off your turning points.

2. DISENGAGE FROM YOUR PAST

Before you can effectively earn the next phase of your life, you have to disengage from the old phase you claim to have left behind. You not only have to let go of past achievements (you are not the person who earned those achievements), you also have to relinquish your old identity and way of doing things. It's okay to learn from our past, but I don't recommend going back to visit every day.

When I first met Curtis Martin in 2018, it had been twelve years since he'd retired from the NFL. I was curious about how he handled the transition from pro athlete to civilian. What did he miss? What had been difficult to let go? I expected him to mention the competition, his teammates, the cheering, the usual stuff we hear in postgame interviews. Silly me. I wasn't close.

Curtis said he missed the "patterns" of being a professional athlete. Players who make it to the NFL tend to be the best athlete in a generation from their high school. Since their early teens, they are noticed, coached, and cared for by well-intentioned adults. They never have to ask for direction from their elders; it is always coming their way, even when they are wealthy superstars in their thirties with minds of their own. From summer camp in July to the playoffs in January, every minute of an NFL player's day is programmed and regimented: what to eat, when to work out, when to study film and memorize the playbook, when to practice, when to take therapy for injuries, when to show up for the team bus or jet. It is not surprising that the most productive players come to correlate some portion of their success with the patterns of training and working they've adopted for so many years.

This is where the Every Breath Paradigm— "Every breath I take is a new me"—asserted itself for Curtis. Maybe it's his awareness of the fragility of an athlete's career, that you're only as good as your last game and you can't rely on last season's statistics to keep your job. Maybe it's something coach Bill Parcells told him: "Curtis, you never want to take yourself out of the game—because the guy replacing you may never let you back on the field." But Curtis lives in the present, with his eye on the future. His past is always behind him, a relic he regards as a previous Curtis. Throughout his playing days, Curtis was operating on two tracks: Curtis the player and Curtis the former player. On the "player track" he adhered to the patterns he was given, knowing they provided the focus that led to success. On the "former player track" he was repurposing the lessons of football in real time into wisdom he could use for the rest of his life. When he retired at thirty-three, it wasn't difficult for him to let go of his need for external direction—because he was ready to replace it with self-direction that came from within him (and that aligned with his larger aspiration, namely, to help others). He still needed "patterns" in his life, but now they were of his own making.

When we are able to disengage from our previous selves, letting go of all the patterns from our past to create a new self becomes as easy as turning off the lights when we leave a room.

3. MASTER THE "EARNING RESPONSE"

There's no mystery to how we form a good habit. It's a well-researched behavioral concept these days, commonly described as a three-step sequence of Stimulus, Response, and Outcome. My teachers in graduate school referred to it as the ABC sequence, for Antecedent, Behavior, and Consequence. I've heard others describe it as the Cause-Action-Effect sequence. Whatever the nomenclature, only the middle part of the sequence matters: our response (or behavior or action). That's the part we can control and change.

If we respond poorly every time to the same stimulus, we shouldn't be surprised that we get the same disappointing outcome each time. Eventually our poor response becomes predictable; we've acquired another poor habit. The only way to eliminate the new habit is to consciously change our response to the unchanging stimulus with better behavior, e.g. instead of "killing the messenger" who brings us bad news, why not remain calm and thank the messenger? Change the response, then change the habit.

I've made a career out of reminding very intelligent leaders of this precept. I tell them to treat any meeting with their staff as a minefield of dangerous stimuli that can bring out their most counterproductive habits: having to be the smartest person in the room; adding too much value; winning every argument; punishing candor. My clients are quick studies. They don't need clinical therapy, just a reminder to be alert to their responses in a meeting. That reminder can be as simple as an index card set in front of them containing words that address their particular issue: *Stop trying to win. Is it worth it? Are you the expert on this topic?* Keeping the card in their line of vision is all they need to do to alter their response to an annoying stimulus. This is how good behavior is ritualized and repeated and transformed into a lasting habit.

Can this same dynamic apply to something as complex and consequential as living an earned life? Can we turn earning into a habit—as automatic as saying "Thank you" to a compliment?

I say yes, as long as we add a thoughtful pause between the stimulus and the outcome before we make our official response. The pause gives us time to consider both the explicit and implicit message of the triggering event, as well as the desired outcome of any action we take. It pushes us to respond rationally, in our best interest, rather than emotionally or impulsively.

In hindsight, on the rare occasions in my school years when someone told me "You can be more," I must have intuited that I was being presented with a meaningful transition in my life. A chance to shed the old Marshall and become someone new. The statement itself was the stimulus, telling me "You're blowing it, kid!" while implying "If you don't change, you'll regret it for the rest of your life." The first time it happened, when Mr. Newton said I was better than a D student, my response was to earn his approval by proving him right. I got straight A's in math my senior year and scored my high school's first perfect 800 on the math achievement test. I'd like to say my response induced a permanent change in attitude. But a single event doesn't create a good habit. Repetition does.

I reverted to my slacker ways in my undergraduate years at Rose-Hulman Institute of Technology in Terre Haute, Indiana. Then it happened again in 1970, this time with Professor Ying in economics class. Dr. Ying expressed great faith in my future if I "cleaned up my act." He encouraged me to take the GMATs and apply to the MBA program at Indiana University, which miraculously brought me into the Ph.D. program at UCLA. There I was on the receiving end of at least two "You can be more" speeches, from professors Bob Tannenbaum and Fred Case. Each time, I responded positively by stepping up my game. By the time I got to my turning point with Paul Hersey, I had repeated my response to the "You can be more" speech enough times that it was practically a habit. Each time, the main driver was my fear that I would regret doing anything less. I was no longer an incorrigible slacker. The desire to maximize my effort to earn my future and avoid the pain of regret had become my earning response.

I believe this is why I've responded so eagerly and aggressively to the times since the late 1970s when I've heard the YCBM speech. I pause to review the factors that necessitated the speech, knowing immediately why they sound so familiar. My brain tells me, "I've been here before. I know the signs. This is a turning point." The stimulus is the same. The reward of a successful outcome is the same. So my response should be the same. My brain races to adjust—and I commit to beginning the next phase of my life. Like everything else, I know it will have to be earned. And I'm okay with that. Thus earning becomes a habit.

It's no different for you, even if you haven't been the lucky beneficiary of as much externally generated encouragement as I have. The truth is, I was so settled in my comfort zone and stunted by inertia that I had to rely on others to push me out of my bubble and start earning my next beginning.

That doesn't have to be you. The YCBM routine isn't just for people who are falling short of their potential. It's for people who have already earned fulfillment but still believe there are higher levels to reach for. Unlike me, you don't have to wait for someone to come along and point you in the right direction (although it's always nice when that happens). You may already be doing it for yourself. Whenever you think you could and should be doing more in your life, you are, in effect, initiating the YCBM drill. Just because it's a self-administered pep talk doesn't make it less valid—or unworthy of becoming a habit.

4. PLAY THE SHOT IN FRONT OF YOU

Golf is such a difficult game that a few miscues over eighteen holes are unavoidable, even for the greatest players on their best day. The best players compensate for that with a well-honed sense of amnesia on the course. They deal briefly and efficiently with the inevitable errors—a quick burst of anger or self-loathing to release the tension—and then it's forgotten. As they take the two-hundred-plus strides between the tee box and the unfortunate spot where their ball has landed—in some cases, twenty or more yards off the fairway in high thick grass with low-hanging tree limbs blocking their path to the green—they are able to clear their mind and narrow their focus onto the ball, the situation, and the shot in front of them. They are masters of being present. Whatever has happened before on the course does not intrude on their thinking. They huddle with their caddie about strategy, yardage, and club selection. They weigh the likelihood of making good contact with the ball buried in high grass. They calculate the risk-reward odds of attempting a heroic shot to the green or taking their medicine and punching the ball back to the fairway. They'll deal with the next shot when they have to, but in the moment they have to decide on the shot they want to play—and hit the ball. Nothing else matters. They do this sixty to seventy times a round. It is part of their routine before every shot. In other words, it is a habit.

The most instructive part of the routine is the walk from the previous position on the course to the next shot, whether it's a 320-yard drive or a twenty-foot putt that stopped three feet short of the hole. Covering that distance is how they transition from the previous shot to the shot at hand—and stay in the moment. If they do this consistently over every shot, they'll be happy about the round, whether or not the scorecard reflects the quality of their play. At least they have the satisfaction of knowing they did all they could under the circumstances.

To a very poor golfer like me (so poor that I gave up the game twenty-five years ago), watching this time-consuming assessment ritual on every shot during a golf telecast is like watching grass grow. Why don't the pros just walk up to the ball and hit it like I used to do? The pros' way is the right way, of course. Sticking to the routine is a big part of what makes them so good. It's also why the pros' approach is such an apt analogue for how we separate the previous and future versions of ourselves from who we are right now. It reinforces the wisdom of being present.

The Nobel Prize winner Daniel Kahneman famously said, "What you see is all there is"—spawning the widely adopted acronym WYSIATI—to point out how quickly we use the limited information at our disposal to make premature conclusions. It was yet another example of humans behaving as biased irrational actors, in this case rushing to judgment.

I prefer to apply his WYSIATI in a more positive light, as a reminder that every set of facts we see is situational—and there's something noble in dealing as best we can with what's in front of us. When golfers play the shot in front of them, they are being supremely rational and disinterested actors, divorced from past or future concerns that may cloud their judgment. They accept that golf, like most of life, is situational, never involving the moment before or after, only now. At their best, they are Buddhist masters of mindfulness and being present.

The enormous value of being present shouldn't be a controversial idea. And yet failing to "play the shot" is one of our most consistent behavior patterns. We do it all day long—when we ignore our kids at the breakfast table because we're mentally rehearsing our presentation later in the day; when we're distracted throughout a meeting because we're reliving a disturbing call ten minutes earlier; when we typecast people by our memory of their worst moments, refusing to forgive them or accept that people change.

When we fail to play the shot in front of us, we are failing at transition. We are failing to see that something in our world, big or small, has changed irrevocably and we have to deal with the new reality. I saw this in the 100 Coaches community when the COVID lockdowns began in March 2020. While some members were able to shift gears smoothly from *that was then* to *this is now,* others were grinding their gears. One of the latter was Tasha Eurich, for whom 2020 had been shaping up as a breakout year. Two years earlier she had published her first book, *Insight,* with a major publisher, about the difference between how we see ourselves and how others see us. The book had gained a lot of traction in the corporate world. Tasha was a dynamic speaker, so good that I asked her to kick off the first afternoon session at our 100 Coaches gathering in San Diego in January 2020. She rocked the house. Six weeks later, everyone's big plans collapsed. Tasha took it hard. She'd spent two years building up to 2020—and now it was all wiped out. The fact that her peers were suffering equally provided no comfort. This was an exogenous shock with no end in sight.

When I checked up on her in early May 2020, she was still haunted by the futility of all her hard work, not ready to move on and face the reality of her situation. The world had changed and she was having trouble transitioning into it. I advised her in play-the-shot thinking and letting go of a past she couldn't change. I also reminded her that the world might have collapsed, but it had not disappeared. Gradually, as her corporate clients acclimated to a new working environment—empty offices, everyone online at home, the rise of Zoom—demand for her expertise came back. It wouldn't be as reliable as before (not yet at least), but slowly she began to leave the past behind. When you do that, all that remains is the present moment and your future. The distinction between the now Tasha and the future Tasha was a meaningful insight for her. It was her escape into a more hopeful situation.

By November 2020, with her consulting and coaching business still short of full capacity, she decided to use her spare time to form her own mentoring community. Emulating the model I'd established with 100 Coaches, she posted a short selfie video inviting applicants to be coached by her. Of the several hundred responses, she selected ten members, nicknaming them the Tasha Ten. There was no money in it and no public acclaim. It was a private act of generosity that added a little more purpose and meaning to her life. She didn't know where it would lead, but she was eager to find out.

That's the moment Tasha's transition was complete. She was no longer clinging to a pre-COVID world that had served her well but was never coming back, and she had found something meaningful to replace it. She had earned her next beginning.

I BEGAN THIS chapter with two questions: *When does earning begin? When does it end?* The short answer: Earning ends when we accomplish what we set out to do, or when changing circumstances in the world or in ourselves make it unnecessary to continue what we've been doing. Earning begins when we decide we need to recreate our life, making it our own even if it's someone else's idea, in order to redefine who we are. In between the beginning and end, we must let go of many things—our role, our identity, our allegiance to the past, our expectations—and then scratch and claw to find our next new thing. This is how we earn each new beginning in our life. We must close the door on one part of our life and open a new door.

EXERCISE

What's Your "Impossible"?

When the poet Donald Hall asked his friend, the sculptor Henry Moore, for the secret to life, Moore, who had just turned eighty, provided a quick, pragmatic answer: "The secret of life is to have a task, something you devote your entire life to, something you bring everything to, every minute of the day for your whole life. And the most important thing is—it must be something you cannot possibly do!" (To me this is the perfect example of aspiration.)

Hall believed that Moore's definition of "something you cannot possibly do" was "to be the greatest sculptor who ever lived and know it." A lofty aspiration, perhaps, but no higher than the seemingly ordinary desires many people harbor: to be happy or enlightened or remembered fondly after we shuffle off this mortal coil.

What's your "something you cannot possibly do"?

CHAPTER 13

PAYING THE PRICE AND EATING MARSHMALLOWS

———————

Some years ago I was one of the speakers at a Women in Business conference hosted by the private wealth group at the Swiss bank UBS. The speaker preceding me was a pioneering female in the tech industry, the founder and CEO of her own company and something of a celebrity. Twenty years later I still remember the wisdom and refreshing candor of what she said. She was a hard act to follow.

She said she didn't conduct mentoring sessions too often, because running a company was a demanding job and she'd be spending all her time mentoring women if she accepted every invitation that came her way. She said she stuck to the three things in life that mattered to her. She spent time with her family. She took care of her health and fitness. And she tried to be great at her job. Those three roles ate up all her bandwidth. She didn't cook, do housework, or run errands. Having grabbed the full attention of every woman in the room, she doubled down on her blunt message: "If you don't like cooking, don't cook. If you don't like gardening, don't garden. If you don't like cleaning up, hire someone to clean up. Only do what is core to you. Everything else, get rid of it."

A woman in the audience raised her hand, declaring, "That's easy for you to say. You're rich."

The CEO wasn't buying that excuse. She pushed back, saying,

"I happen to know that the lowest salary in this room is a quarter of a million dollars. None of you would be invited here if you weren't doing well. Are you telling me that you can't afford to hire someone to do the stuff you don't want to do? You wouldn't accept minimum wage as a professional. Why is it okay anywhere else? You are totally devaluing your time."

She was delivering a hard truth that's tough for many people to accept: *To pursue any kind of fulfilling life, especially an earned life, you have to pay a price.* She wasn't talking about money. She was talking about making the maximum effort on the important things, accepting the necessary sacrifices, being aware of the risks and the specter of failure but being able to block them out.

Some of us are willing to pay that price. Others are not, for reasons that are compelling but also, when all is said and done, regrettable.

One of the more common excuses is a variation on the well-known concept of loss aversion—our impulse to avoid a loss is greater than our desire to acquire an equivalent gain. We are willing to pay the price when there's a high probability that our efforts will achieve success, far less eager when the probability is low. We want certainty that our effort and sacrifice will not be in vain. We are terrorized by the prospect of putting everything we have into achieving a goal and ending up with nothing to show for it. Total commitment shouldn't be a futile gesture, we think. It's not fair. So we avoid paying that price. No commitment, no futility.

This is such a powerful belief that I've come to accommodate it in my one-on-one coaching, even though my successful clients are demonstrably comfortable with paying the price. It's what got them where they are. Yet I still feel the need to assure them that their commitment to the coaching process will not be futile. "This is hard," I say. "One slipup can undo your progress and send you back to square one. But if you follow up and stick with it for the next year or two, you *will* get better." It's as close as I'm willing to go to offering a guarantee, but imparting my certainty is part of the coaching. In reducing my clients' resistance to paying the price, I'm giving them a head start on success.

Another reason is a failure of vision. Our sacrifice today does not yield a reward we can enjoy today. The benefit from our self-control is far down the road, bequeathed to a future version of us whom we do not know. It's why we'd rather spend our spare cash on ourselves now than save it and let the wonders of compound interest turn it into a useful sum thirty years later. Some people can pay that price, foreseeing the future gratitude they'll feel toward their former self who sacrificed in their interest. Some people can't see that far ahead.

A third reason is our zero-sum view of the world, in which winning something here means losing something there. Paying the price is an opportunity cost, calculated in what we must sacrifice. If I do this, I can't do that. This view isn't entirely wrong. It's merely pointless as a consideration about paying the price. When we choose to pay the price—that is, do something challenging and risky rather than an easy sure thing—it doesn't follow that we have sacrificed the sure thing. Most times, when you choose the difficult path, you've automatically eliminated all other options, including the sure thing. After all, you can't be in two places at the same time; something's got to give. The sooner you accept that, the more comfortable you'll be about paying the price. I remember reading a story about the great French skier Jean-Claude Killy pointing out to his manager, "I train wherever it's winter. Half the year in the Northern Hemisphere, half in the Southern Hemisphere. I haven't experienced summer in years." Killy, a French national hero and the dominant athlete at the 1968 Winter Olympics, where he swept all the gold medals in alpine skiing, wasn't describing the absence of summers as a hardship he suffered. He was stating that he was comfortable with the price he paid to be world champion. He could experience summer as much as he wanted after he put his gold medals away.

In recent years I've noticed a fourth reason people hesitate to pay the price for earning anything: It forces them out of their comfort zone. For example, I don't like confrontation and avoid it nine out of ten times. It just isn't worth it to me. But that tenth time, when something I value greatly is in jeopardy (a project, my family, a friend in need), I'm willing to confront anyone to do what I think is necessary. I don't enjoy doing it, but I don't regret having done it.

I'm not mocking these reasons. When the price you have to pay grossly outweighs the anticipated reward, any of these reasons sounds like common sense. The required effort is simply not worth the result. It's like devoting six months to learning a foreign language for a one-day visit to the country where it's spoken. Better to hire an interpreter for the day.

To make smarter choices about when to pay the price and when to pass, we first have to resolve the omnipresent dichotomy of delayed gratification versus instant gratification. In my dictionary, *paying the price* may as well be a synonym for *delayed gratification* (and *not paying the price* is a synonym for *instant gratification*). They're both about self-control. It's a dilemma you face each day and all day, from the moment you wake up. For example, you want to get up early to exercise before heading off to work. When the alarm goes off at 5:45 A.M., you pause for a moment, tempted by the instant gratification of staying in bed for another half hour of sleep, weighing it against the benefit of your fitness routine as well as the psychic pain of starting your day with an episode of defeated intention, a galling failure of will and purpose. Whether or not the workout triumphs over sleep, this is just the first of many times you'll have to resolve the delayed versus instant gratification dichotomy today. It continues at breakfast. Will it be the usual healthful oatmeal and fruit, or the tempting eggs, bacon, and toast with a double latte chaser? Then there's your first hour at work. Will you spend it tackling the toughest item on your to-do list or shooting the breeze with your office neighbors? And so on until day's end, when you must choose between tucking in at a decent hour or staying up late with Netflix. It never stops.

Our attitude about delayed gratification changes in interesting ways from birth to death. As I see it, there are only two times in your adult life when instant gratification isn't a choice that tortures the soul. The first is in your early years of adulthood, when you have no sense of disappearing time. You don't see the need to save your money or take care of your health or, for that matter, devote yourself to a specific career. You can be extravagant with your time and resources because you have time to make up lost ground. Paying the price is something you can delay till some time "later" (whatever that means). The other time is late in life, when the gap between the now you and the future you narrows. At a certain age you become who you always thought you wanted to be, or, failing that high hurdle, accept who you have actually become. It's time to cash in your chips. So you book the expensive trip. You volunteer your time freely. You eat the quart of ice cream without guilt.

In the many years between, you are constantly tested by delayed gratification. It's why your ability to experience delayed gratification is such a decisive factor in living an earned life, perhaps an even more reliable predictor than intelligence.

In the end, the most persuasive reason for paying the price is that anytime you sacrifice for something, you are compelled to value it more. Adding value to your life is a goal worth earning. Then again, paying the price also feels good, whether or not your heroic effort delivered the reward. There's no shame in falling short if you gave it your best shot.

There's no regret either. Regret is the price you pay for not paying the price.

THAT SAID, THERE are times in our active lives when we can legitimately feel we've paid enough—and should luxuriate, however briefly, in easing up on ourselves. A marshmallow is calling us.

In the late 1960s, the Stanford psychologist Walter Mischel conducted his famous "marshmallow studies" with preschool children at the university's Bing Nursery School. Children were shown one marshmallow and told they could choose to eat the marshmallow whenever they wanted. They were also told that a larger reward of two marshmallows (the menu of treats included cookies, mints, mini-pretzels, and more) would be theirs if they waited alone for up to twenty minutes without eating the marshmallow. It was a vivid choice between immediate gratification and delayed gratification. The child would sit alone at a table facing one marshmallow and a desk bell that could be rung at any time to call back the researcher and eat the marshmallow. Or the child could wait for the researcher to return, as much as twenty minutes later, and, if the marshmallow remained uneaten, receive two marshmallows. Mischel wrote:

> The struggles we observed as these children tried to restrain themselves from ringing the bell could bring tears to your

eyes, have you applauding their creativeness and cheering them on, and give you fresh hope for the potential of even young children to resist temptation and persevere for their delayed rewards.

Follow-up research on the children years later led Mischel to conclude that the subjects who waited for the two marshmallows had higher SAT scores, better educational achievement, and lower body mass index. These studies eventually led to Mischel's 1994 book, *The Marshmallow Test: Why Self-Control Is the Engine of Success,* establishing the test as one of the rare laboratory studies about human behavior that has become a cultural touchstone (e.g. T-shirts saying "Don't Eat the Marshmallow").*

Broadly defined, delayed gratification means resisting smaller, pleasurable rewards now for larger, more significant rewards later. Much of the psychology literature deifies delayed gratification, linking it with all we associate with "achievement." We are relentlessly bombarded with the virtue of sacrificing immediate pleasure to achieve long-term results.

But there's another way to look at the Marshmallow Test. Although the study's implied learning—delayed gratification is unilaterally good—is hard to ignore, imagine if the study was extended beyond the second marshmallow. After waiting the

---

* Later studies, applying common sense, questioned the soundness of the original test. Affluent kids with highly educated parents in the Stanford University community were more likely to be brought up in an environment where the rewards from delayed gratification were more obvious than what poor kids with less educated parents were used to. These children were also more likely to believe that the authority figure—the experimenter—would deliver the reward.

required minutes, the child was given a second marshmallow but told, "If you wait a little longer, you will get a third marshmallow!" And a fourth marshmallow . . . a fifth marshmallow . . . a hundredth marshmallow.

By that logic, the ultimate master of delayed gratification would be an old person near death in a room surrounded by thousands of stale uneaten marshmallows. It's safe to say that none of us would want to be that person when we're old and dying.

I often strike this cautionary note about the marshmallows with my coaching clients. Their level of achievement is awe-inspiring as is their willpower and mastery of delayed gratification. My coaching clients have included many of the most successful leaders in the world. They often have impressive educations. Sometimes they're so busy making sacrifices to achieve for the future that they forget to enjoy life now. My advice to them is my advice to you: *Know that there are times when you should eat the marshmallow. Then, eat the marshmallow!* Do it today (if only to recover the thrill of instant gratification). Don't wait for some late-life glimpse-of-mortality event to shake you up.

The business writer John Byrne (full disclosure: I officiated at his wedding), who collaborated with Jack Welch on his 2001 memoir, *Jack: Straight from the Gut,* told me a story about Welch after his heart attack and triple bypass surgery at age fifty-nine in 1995. The surgery scared Welch into rethinking things big and small about his life. One lesson? Quit drinking cheap wine. Welch had been CEO of General Electric for fourteen years by then and was a wealthy man, but you wouldn't know it from the inexpensive wine he had been serving at home. With his heightened awareness of life's brevity, Welch filled his cellar with nothing but the most precious Bordeaux reds from then on. If you were dining with Welch at home, this is all he served. Basically, you were drinking a lucky man's marshmallows.

In creating a great life for yourself, accept the fact that long-term achievement requires short-term sacrifice. But don't go overboard on delayed gratification. Stop to enjoy the journey. Life is a perpetual marshmallow test, but there's no medal for accumulating the most uneaten marshmallows. You might as well be hoarding regrets.

Late in his book, Walter Mischel tells a contrasting tale of two brothers. One is a serious and wealthy investment banker with a long, stable marriage and adult children who are doing well. The other brother is a writer living in Greenwich Village who has published five novels that have barely been noticed by the reading public but who "described himself nevertheless as having a great time, spending his days writing and living the bachelor life at night, going from one short-term relationship to the next." The writer, referencing the Marshmallow Test, speculates that his earnest straight-laced banker brother is capable of waiting forever for his marshmallows, in sharp contrast to the writer, who regards instant gratification as a lifestyle choice.

Surprisingly, Mischel employs the brotherly contrast to give his blessing to the writer's life, pointing out that the writer must have developed great self-control to make it through creative writing courses in college and then actually produce five novels. Mischel also excuses the writer's free-spirited dating life, noting that the writer probably needed the same self-control "to maintain his fun relationships while staying uncommitted."

In other words, the man who invented the Marshmallow Test wants all of us to eat some marshmallows too.

EXERCISE

Take the Delay out of Delayed Gratification

This is an exercise to become more aware about the role delayed gratification plays in our lives.

DO THIS: For one full day, filter every dilemma you face through the dichotomy of delayed gratification (not eating the marshmallow) versus instant gratification (eating it). Facing any either/or decision, pause for seven seconds (a brief delay anyone can handle) and then ask yourself, *Can I delay gratification at this moment for the sake of a higher reward in the future, or am I taking the easy way out and settling for instant gratification?* Put another way: *Am I paying the price in this situation, or am I cashing in?*

If you find that the exercise makes you more alert to delayed gratification's rewards and your capacity to meet the challenge—at least more than if you mindlessly surrendered to instant gratification—try to stick with it as long as you can. It's not easy. It's a lot of self-monitoring, considering all the temptations we face each day. But like sticking with a diet or a fitness routine, if you can make it through the first four or five days without quitting, you've improved the odds that delayed gratification can become your default response rather than a remarkable event. Do that and you're ready for an advanced exercise.

NOW DO THIS: All of us create hierarchies in our minds for our goals. Some we give high priority, some low. Some are hard to achieve, some are easy. In my experience, the hard goals tend to be the high-priority items, the easy ones the low-priority. Conventional wisdom says we should start each day getting the easy, low-priority goals out of the way, because it's nice to begin the day with some victories. And because we're human, naturally drawn to the low-hanging fruit of easy goals, we follow the conventional wisdom, all the while delaying the gratification of tackling our high-priority goals.

For one day, be unconventional. Tackle the high-priority goal first.

Like any suggestion that defies convention, this onetime task (it's only for one day) can be a challenge for most of us—precisely because our high-priority goals tend to be high in difficulty. For example, I try to answer every piece of correspondence I get—requests, invitations, suggestions, positive or negative comments, either analog or digital—within two days of receipt. I don't like to ignore people who take the time to write to me; they deserve a response. It's not particularly urgent and rarely consequential, nor do I relish spending three hours every other day sending notes and emails to people I've never met. But answering correspondence is nowhere near as challenging as writing a chapter of a book. So when I feel the need to continue working into the evening rather than call it a day, I'll turn to the letters and emails rather than what I tell myself is a higher-priority goal such as writing for two hours. In my hierarchy of things to do, answering mail is easy, a medium priority; writing is a heavy lift and a very high priority. In choosing the easy task before I call it a day, I cannot honestly say I'm experiencing or earning any delayed gratification, because answering correspondence is nowhere near as gratifying as finishing the next chapter. (There's no delayed gratification if I'm not gratified.) So how much of a price am I really paying?

Were writing really as high a priority as I claim it is, I would adopt the strategy of many successful writers with greater self-control than I possess. They do their writing first thing in the morning, when their mind is rested and before anything else can distract them. Whether their plan is to stay at their desk for five uninterrupted hours or hit a specific word count, if they stick to the plan, they get the extreme gratification of starting each day with their biggest accomplishment. Their first thing is the earned thing. Everything that follows is a bonus.

This is such an appealing benefit it's stunning that most of us (including me) don't copy the practice. Through the rinse-and-repeat regularity of showing up at their desk to write first thing in the morning, these writers have taken the delay out of delayed gratification. They have their marshmallow and eat it too (right after they finish for the day).

CHAPTER 14

CREDIBILITY MUST
BE EARNED TWICE

W hat is the purpose of living an earned life?

One answer I admire comes from Peter Drucker, who said, "Our mission in life is to make a positive difference, not to prove how smart or right we are."

We alone define how we make a positive difference. Some people do it on a grand scale of sacrifice and ambition: doctors saving lives, activists righting wrongs, philanthropists reshaping society. Others do it with humble, small-scale gestures: going out of our way to comfort a friend in pain, coaching Little League, introducing two people who end up falling in love, being the parent our children need. In between these extremes, there are the myriad commonplace good deeds that create a legacy of thoughtfulness and kindness.

When I have asked successful people to characterize the fulfillment they get from pursuing an earned life, the number one answer by far is some variation of "helping people." I regard these responses as confirmation yet again (if any more were needed) of Peter Drucker's piercing but generous insight about us. In stating that "Our mission in life is to make a positive difference," he wasn't exhorting us to do the right thing; he was describing what is already there, what we already know about ourselves. We most fully earn our life when we are of service to others.*

To understand the kind of positive impact you want to make in your life, you need to come to terms with two deeply personal qualities. The first is credibility, the other is empathy. You need both to make a positive difference. In this chapter, we'll explore the importance of credibility.

CREDIBILITY IS A reputational quality earned over time when people trust you and believe what you say.

Earning credibility is a two-step process. The first step is establishing your competence in something that other people value—and doing it well on a consistent basis. This is how you gain other people's trust. They know you will deliver what you promise. The second step is gaining other people's recognition and approval for your particular competence. You need both trust and approval to credibly credit yourself with credibility. For example, if you are a saleswoman who tops her quota month after month, people eventually take notice. Continue your unblemished streak for a year or two, and you acquire credibility. Consistent competency creates

---

* Even a few of the more I-centric runner-up answers are tinted in the tonalities of making a positive difference: "providing for my family" and "raising my kids to be healthy productive citizens," more so perhaps than "building a business" or "making enough money to retire at fifty." But if you dig deeper to understand any individual's source of fulfillment, I suspect you'll see that making a positive difference is usually a part of it. My client Harry Kraemer, for example, was fifty years old in 2005 when he retired as CEO of Baxter Pharmaceuticals in Chicago. He didn't need or want another CEO job. Instead, he became one of the most popular professors at Northwestern's Kellogg School of Business, making an impact on hundreds of students that, in his mind, matched his previous good work producing life-saving medicines at Baxter.

credibility. Credibility creates influence. It is the earned authority that helps us persuade people to do right, which in turn increases our ability to make a positive difference.

The path from competence to making a positive difference is fairly direct. Assuming a person's goodwill, competence combined with recognition for it leads to credibility, which leads to influence, which leads to making a positive difference. It's certainly true with my hero-mentors, such as Paul Hersey, Frances Hesselbein, and Peter Drucker. They had years of steady accomplishment to make their mark and be admired (aka approved) for it, long before I appeared in their lives. Their obvious hypercompetency was the source of their profound influence on me and why my desire to be associated with them was a no-brainer. But that was just the opening move. The positive difference they made in my life was so great, I soon realized I wanted to be like them, especially if the kind of credibility they had earned could be mine as well. I can't think of a more profound or gratifying form of approval than achieving an earned life that other people—your children, students, colleagues, acolytes, readers—want to earn too.

I committed to this goal more than twenty-five years ago. I already knew that credibility was critical to succeeding at being an executive coach, particularly if I was narrowing my client base to people at the top of the corporate ladder. At the highest levels, clients need to know not only that you're competent but that people the clients respect approve of you. That's the first time I realized that credibility has to be earned twice—initially when I reached a high level of competency, then a second time while I waited for people to notice my growing ability and accord me the recognition that leads to credibility.

Many years later, on one of our LPR calls in 2020, Safi Bahcall, a polymathic physicist, entrepreneur, and author of *Loonshots,* would offer a revelation that perfectly described my challenge with earning credibility. Safi was struggling to accurately score his effort on achieving happiness each week on the LPR call, until he realized why measuring happiness confused him so much. He was associating achievement with happiness—i.e., achieving a goal should make him happy, and conversely, being happy should improve his ability to achieve a goal—when in fact they are independent variables on the road to having a good life and making a positive difference. They may be correlated, but not necessarily so. Earning happiness is a pursuit in itself, independent from earning any achievement. Our experience tells us that being happy doesn't deliver achievement and, vice versa, achievement doesn't always deliver happiness. After all, many high achievers are miserable or depressed.

In the same way that achievement and happiness were independent variables, earning competence did not automatically guarantee that I would be recognized for it. Greater competence and recognition for it are two independent variables that I would have to connect for others to see. To acquire larger credibility as a coach, I would have to become well known. This recognition would not be given to me. I would have to get out of my comfort zone of "just doing the work" by adding a new essential task to my definition of "just doing the work"—namely, becoming better known. My good work was no longer going to "speak for itself." That hubris may have worked fifty years ago, in simpler times. But in a so-called Attention Economy where being noticed is a full-contact sport, it's an incomplete strategy. You're declaring victory with the job half done. You not only have to tell a good story that speaks for itself, you have to sell your ability at storytelling. The awkwardness often associated with self-marketing—whether you're seeking attention for an achievement at work or you want to get your new start-up noticed—is the new additional price you have to pay for success in a rapidly changing environment. It's less discomfiting if you can reasonably argue that accepting the awkward duties of self-marketing serves the aspirational purpose of making a positive difference. This has become a telling part of my coaching now, but first I had to test it on myself. I conducted a Socratic dialogue with four questions:

1. If I became more widely recognized as an expert on coaching executives, could I make more of a positive difference in the world?
2. Does striving for this recognition make me uncomfortable?
3. Does my discomfort inhibit me and therefore limit my ability to make a positive difference?
4. Which is more important to me: my momentary discomfort or making a positive difference?

When I can convince myself that any uncomfortable task is for a greater good, my discomfort suddenly becomes a price that I'm happy to pay.

I HAVE A confession to make brought on by mention of our discomfiture with seeking recognition. From the opening pages of this book, I have earnestly avoided depicting an earned life exclusively through the blunt calculus of choice, risk, and effort leading to an earned reward. It's certainly part of the picture, but first and foremost our earning must serve a higher aspiration. It's not merely about results.

I confess now to a grave sin of omission. I have failed to address the absolute certainty that we won't get what we want simply because we strive for it, even when our choices are unimpeachable, our efforts flawless and complete. I omitted the possibility that the world isn't always fair to us. If it were, none of us would ever feel ignored or ill treated or otherwise victimized. Being good people with noble intentions, committed to making a positive difference, we would get exactly what we deserve.

At this point in our adult lives, we know that people and circumstances are not always so obliging. If you've ever done something wonderful only to have the world ignore it, or even punish you for it, you know this to be true. A lot of times it's not your fault. Your timing was off. Someone else's good work stole your thunder. You were drowned out by a louder voice craving attention.

What's odd is that we see this problem clearly in other people but rarely accept it as reality when it happens to us. If a friend were launching a retail product today, we'd assume she had a complete marketing plan to draw attention to her brand—advertising; a sophisticated social media campaign; free samples to elicit positive reviews; paid placement on store shelves; free media in the form of press releases, interviews, and profiles—all in the pursuit of recognition and approval that results in a little more credibility for her brand. Anything less would be folly with a retail product.

Yet we don't automatically translate this to ourselves at work or anywhere else. We may feel that calling attention to ourselves is unseemly and narcissistic. Our great work should speak for itself. We shouldn't have to do that. I've heard all the excuses, to which I say: You wouldn't go full tilt in the first half of a game and then phone it in for the second half, expecting a successful result, would you? Then why would you behave the same way when the fate of your hard work, your career, your earned life hangs in the balance?

This is why we have to come to terms with credibility. As a personal attribute it is essential to making a positive difference—and living an earned life. Fortunately, I have a plan.

IN ADDITION TO his insight about making a positive difference, Peter Drucker had five other rules that are applicable for earning credibility. At first they may strike you as self-evident, even trite, but smarter people than I have had the same initial reaction and now are quoting them back to me on a regular basis. If you want to elevate your credibility, start by committing these Druckerisms to memory:

1. Every decision in the world is made by the person who has the power to make the decision. Make peace with that.
2. If we need to influence someone in order to make a positive difference, that person is our *customer* and we are a *salesperson*.
3. Our customer does not need to buy; we need to sell.
4. When we are trying to sell, our personal definition of value is far less important than our customer's definition of value.
5. We should focus on the areas where we can actually make a positive difference. Sell what we can sell and change what we can change. Let go of what we cannot sell or change.

Each of these rules assumes that acquiring recognition and approval is a transactional exercise. Note the frequent reference to selling and customers. The implication is that we must sell our achievements and competence in order to have them recognized and appreciated by others. These Druckerisms not only endorse our need for approval, they emphasize that we can't afford to be passive about it—not when our credibility is at stake.

But there is a right way to seek approval and a wrong way. Since our earliest days, when we were trying to please our parents, we have spent our lives seeking approval from people who could influence our future. It continued in school when we sought our teachers' approval, then increased in intensity when our bosses and customers became the decision makers who held sway over our livelihood. (See rule 1.) The higher we climb, the more proficient we become at proving ourselves. Eventually it becomes second nature; we don't realize that we are doing it. That's when we start making mistakes that damage our credibility rather than enhance it. The following matrix will help you determine when proving yourself to others is a worthwhile activity—and when it is a waste of time or does more harm than good:

CREDIBILITY MATRIX

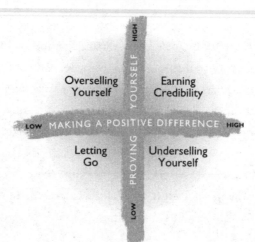

The vertical axis measures one dimension: our level of striving to prove ourselves. The horizontal axis measures a second dimension of credibility: making a positive difference. The matrix illustrates the connections between the two dimensions. We are asking ourselves two questions: (1) Am I striving to prove myself? and (2) Will proving myself help me make a positive difference? The utility of the matrix is situational. In some situations our answers to those questions can be high or low. When both are high or low, we're in a good place.

Let's examine what's at stake in each of these four quadrants and how it determines our behavior.

Earning Credibility: The most beneficial quadrant is in the upper right, where you're proactively seeking approval and it will make a positive difference in your own life or the lives of others. Aggressively seeking a job you know you can do better than anyone else is a good example. Some years ago, one of my coaching clients heard a rumor that he was being passed over for the CEO spot at his company. The job was rumored to be going to an outsider whom my client knew well and regarded as an all-hat-and-no-cattle charlatan. Disappointed as he was, my client was even more worried for the future of the company with this phony in charge.

"Has it been announced yet?" I asked. No.

"Do you believe you're a better choice?" Yes.

"Then it's just a rumor," I said. "That's your opening to fight for the job."

He wrote a twenty-eight-page proposal detailing his plans for the company and sent it to the chairman of the board (and alerted his boss), asking for a meeting to plead his case. At the meeting, the chairman of the board told him that he had indeed been passed over because he wasn't perceived as having a "fire in the belly" for leading the company. His gumption to write the proposal and sell himself directly to the chairman—the decision maker who had the power to choose the next CEO—reversed that opinion. He got the job.

This is the quadrant you want to be in—selling yourself with no fear—when your competency is not in doubt and the outcome will make a positive difference across the board. Anything less would be regrettable.

Letting Go: This is the "It's Not Worth It" quadrant, where straining to prove yourself will not make a positive difference and you don't feel any need for approval. Arguing politics with someone who is diametrically opposed to your position and unwilling to be moved by anything you say is a common example. Instead of banging your head against a wall with your "opponent," you should be asking yourself, "Is this worth it?" The answer is invariably no, and you have to let it go. I find myself in this quadrant a few times every day. It happens when I'm asked for my opinion on a topic on which I have limited knowledge, which could be anything from corporate strategy to macroeconomics to cooking. I've learned the hard, painful way that any uninformed opinion I offered could do more harm than good if it's taken seriously. This would not make a positive difference. I rely now on a standard three-word response: "Not an expert." This ends the conversation, respecting and protecting all involved.

Although both the conditions here are negative, this is the other good quadrant to be in. A double negative, after all, is a positive. When you're not trying to prove yourself and it won't make a positive difference if you were, your only acceptable response is letting go. Anything else is wasted time.

Underselling Yourself: This is the "I Shouldn't Have to . . ." quadrant, where earning approval would improve your credibility and make a positive difference but you are unwilling to prove yourself. Sometimes it's the excess ego where you believe your ability speaks for itself, that your reputation is your sales pitch. So you hold back when you should be putting your best foot forward.

Sometimes it's too little ego. You have self-doubt or feel like an impostor (you believe the competence attributed to you is not merited and you don't deserve approval). You're not expressing the confidence you should have.

Overselling Yourself: This is the "Tone Deaf" quadrant, where the chances of making a positive difference are low to nil and yet your need for approval is jumping off the charts. You commit the sin of overselling. You're trying to win a game that no one else is playing.

This, too, is rooted in too much or too little ego. When we're underconfident, we compensate by overselling ourselves. This is the most common feedback I hear from board members when inexperienced people make presentations to the board. They often talk too much and overexplain. It's the same with excessively confident people. They talk too much, overexplain, and try too hard to prove themselves. Whatever the reason, overselling rarely makes a positive difference or improves our credibility.

When you oversell yourself, you're breaking all of Peter Drucker's rules. You're not trying to make a positive difference, because it's not an option in this particular situation. You're selling what you value, not what the customer values. Even worse, you don't know what the customer values. And even worse than that, you're selling to someone who is not the decision maker—the ultimate exercise in futility. The net result is worse than a failure to improve your situation. Instead of staying in place, you've taken a step or two back.

In the past, this was the quadrant I was most likely to fall into when I wasn't paying attention to Drucker's rules. The most egregious moment was in the early 1990s, when I had just returned from an International Red Cross family relief program in Africa. My experience was reported on the front page of the local newspaper, *La Jolla Light*. Dr. Sam Popkin, a revered political science professor at UC San Diego, hosted a party in my honor. He toasted me with effusive praise for my humanitarian efforts. It was a perfect occasion for underselling myself. Sam had provided all the credibility I deserved. And yet that didn't stop me from pointlessly overselling my time in Africa to a small group of neighbors at the party. I was giddy and full of myself, behaving like an overzealous "salesperson" even though there was no evidence that my audience were "customers." As the group dissipated, one older gentleman remained. Finally, I took a breath and said to him, "I'm sorry, I didn't get your name."

He put out his hand to shake mine and said, "I'm Jonas Salk. It's nice to meet you."

Facing the man who invented the polio vaccine, I didn't have to ask, "And what do you do?" His name was his credibility. His credibility was his name.

EACH OF THE four quadrants in the matrix tells you when you should try to seek approval—i.e., sell yourself—and when it's not appropriate. Each of Drucker's points is illustrated somewhere in the matrix. "Overselling" is wasting time and effort trying to prove you're smart or right rather than trying to make a difference. Changing what you can change and letting go of what you cannot change is "Letting Go." Placing more value on your needs than on what the customer needs is "Underselling." In the most optimal box, "Earning Credibility," you'll find all the Druckerisms. You're not only trying to make a positive difference, you also accept your salesperson's role. You value the customer's needs more than your own. You also accept that the customer has the power to make the decision—and you don't question it if it doesn't go your way. You don't try to change what you cannot change.

The Credibility Matrix addresses an issue I've been focused on for years: It's one thing to be competent, it's another thing to be recognized for it. It's not enough to gain credibility with one but not the other. You have to earn it twice. Otherwise, you're diminishing your ability to make a positive difference—and lessening the impact of your life.

EXERCISE

What's Your Big Reveal?

Maybe this has happened to you. You're at a family wedding involving people once or twice removed from your immediate family. You have a breezy familiarity with some of the guests and wedding party members, less so with most of the guests. At the reception, you watch your quiet cousin Ed coaxed onto the dance floor, where you discover that he moves like a cross between Fred Astaire and Justin Timberlake. You're genuinely surprised to learn that Ed is a terrific dancer. Where's he been hiding this talent all his life?

It happens again during the toasts. Erica, the always-serious maid of honor studying for her Ph.D. in chemistry, whom you've known since her childhood, stands up to toast the bride and groom and delivers a ten-minute speech from memory that is both funny and heartfelt, dazzling the room and taking the wedding vibe to another level. As you applaud Erica, you turn to the people at your table, all of you thinking the same thing: *Who knew Erica was so funny?*

The scene is a staple of comedies and thrillers. It's the Big Reveal where we discover that a heretofore unimpressive character has abilities we never suspected. It's learning that Marisa Tomei's character in *My Cousin Vinny,* the sneaky-smart-and-competent Monica Vito, knows a lot about cars. These are movie scenes we can watch repeatedly because they provide such satisfying closure. We are happy to see the character's excellence revealed, perhaps envying that their special quality is finally known to all. I suspect a lot of us feel that way: We yearn for our specialness to be known.

But first we have to identify the special skills and personality traits that very few people know about us.

DO THIS: What about you, when finally out in the open, would surprise people and leave them thinking, "Who knew?" Maybe it's your world-class collection of Arts and Crafts pottery, or that you volunteer at a soup kitchen every Sunday, or that your poetry has been published in serious journals, or that you know how to write code, or that you win your age-group at national Masters Swimming championships. Maybe you're like Ed and Erica—you dance well or can deliver a toast like a professional stand-up—and simply needed a wedding for your Big Reveal.

My point is, once revealed, your Who Knew? quality is an eye-opening experience for other people who thought they knew you, leaving them to infer that you have hidden depths of passion, commitment, and resourcefulness, that you're more capable than they thought. It elevates your credibility in their eyes. It's the ideal net result: You are earning credibility.

Now extend this exercise to the workplace. What is the Big Reveal—your Who Knew? quality—that would raise your credibility among your peers and bosses? If everyone knew, what positive difference would it make in your life? Why are you hiding it?

CHAPTER 15

SINGULAR EMPATHY

*E*mpathy is the second deeply personal quality that shapes our ability to make a positive impact.

Empathy is the act of experiencing what other people are feeling or thinking. A German philosopher created the term in 1873—from the word *Einfühlung,* for "feeling into"—and that's how we think of it nowadays: We feel our way into other people's emotions and situations.

One of the most important qualities of living an earned life is building positive relationships (hence the "Did I do my best to maintain relationships?" question in the LPR). Empathy, I think we all can admit, is one of the most important variables in building relationships. Like most things that matter, it is a discipline that must be learned. Whereas credibility helps us influence others, empathy helps us build positive relationships, but both serve the same purpose—making a positive difference.

We tend to think of empathy as a good thing. What's wrong with being alert to the suffering of others and showing concern? But empathy is not only about feeling another person's pain. It's more complicated than that. Empathy is a highly adaptable human response, changing with each situation. Sometimes we feel it in our head. Sometimes we express it directly from the heart. Sometimes it can overwhelm us physically, rendering us powerless.

Sometimes we express empathy through our impulse to do something. Our empathy shifts shapes as the situation shifts.

My favorite—because it's most useful for a coach—is the empathy of *understanding*, whereby we understand why and how other people think and feel the way that they do. I've heard it called *cognitive empathy*, suggesting that we are capable of occupying the same head space as another person. We understand the other person's motivations. We can predict how they'll react to a decision. Cognitive empathy is why married couples and longtime partners can finish each other's sentences. It's the secret skill that great salespeople rely on to meet their customers' needs, and why a great salesperson's truest boast is "I know my customers." It's the keen understanding, often acquired through market research and product testing, that effective advertisers employ to create messaging that makes us want to buy their products, usually in ways we're not aware of. This type of manipulation, taken too far, calls up the dark side of the empathy of understanding. It's how sinister political actors, understanding the biases and grievances of the citizenry, can sway people to create sociopolitical turmoil and revolution. It's also a reminder that we humans have been underestimating empathy's power, in all its forms, for centuries.

We also possess an empathy of *feeling*—experiencing the emotional state of the other person. It's the empathy we display when we replicate within ourselves the feeling of another person, usually to communicate to that person some variation of either "I feel your pain" or "I am happy for you." It is a powerful force within us. Brain studies of people's reactions to emotional events have shown that rabid sports fans in the United States can experience as intense a joy at seeing their football team score a touchdown as the joy felt by the player who actually scored the touchdown. It's why we cry or laugh while watching movie characters that we know are only acting. When the character on screen is excited or scared, we are excited or scared. It's why we are comforted by a medical doctor's so-called bedside manner; through the doctor's replication of what we're feeling, we learn that we are not alone in our fear or suffering. Parents may feel this form of empathy most intensely, not always with positive effect. I once asked my neighbor Jim, the father of five, why he seemed downcast whenever I saw him. He said, "As a father, I can only be as happy as my least happy child." That's the risk that comes with the empathy of feeling. We can feel too much, to the point where we get lost in another's pain and are hurting rather than helping ourselves as well as the object of our concern. We can reduce this particular risk, says the French empathy expert Hortense le Gentil, with a well-intended come-and-go strategy. "By all means, share the other person's feelings," she says, "but do not stay too long at the party. Join in and then get out."

A more subtle form of empathy appears when we feel concern for the other person's reaction to an event. This empathy of *caring* differs from the empathy of feeling in one important way: It is caused by *concern for the person's reaction to the event, not the event itself.* For example, one of the other fathers at your daughter's soccer team game might feel joy when the team scores, whether his daughter or someone else was responsible for the goal (the goal is a happy event), whereas you might feel joy only at seeing how happy the goal made your daughter feel (not the event but her reaction to the happy event). In the empathy of caring, you are happy or sad because the person is happy or sad, not because the situation is a happy or sad occasion. Family events elicit the empathy of caring all the time. If we enjoy ourselves immensely at a dinner but the evening ends with our spouse upset about something that happened at the party, our pleasure tends to be immediately overwhelmed by our spouse's distress. We are naturally inclined to empathize with our spouse's pain—because who wants a husband, wife, or partner who doesn't care? People in customer-facing businesses are particularly adroit at the empathy of caring, displaying a concern for the customer's displeasure after a mishap rather than the mishap itself. Customers appreciate the empathic gesture; they will forgive almost any error if they see that you care enough about them to fix it.

The most effective empathic gesture is the empathy of *doing*—when you go beyond understanding, feeling, and caring and actually take action to make a difference. It's the extra step, always exacting a cost in some way, that few of us are willing to take. And even when we do act on our empathic feelings, our well-intended actions can be excessive rather than a positive difference maker. When I told my client Joan, a wealthy matriarch of an old-money East Coast dynasty who does an amazing amount of good work for her community and never talks about it, how much I admired her as a positive role model for the empathy of doing, she graciously demurred. "If I'm not careful, I become a fixer. I care too much, then I do too much. So I try to solve other people's problems rather than let them learn from their mistakes and fix it themselves. I become their crutch and end up making them more dependent."

We experience these types of empathy in myriad situations: when we are overwhelmed with concern for society's disadvantaged; when we're alarmed by the choices others make because we've been there, done that; when we employ our understanding of people to get in our way; when we mimic another person's physical discomfort, e.g. copying someone's itch-scratching or stuttering; when we perfectly comprehend a person's emotional struggle because we remember when it happened to us; and so on. We have the opportunity to be empathic dozens of times a day—and each time is an opportunity to display empathy either well or poorly. If you've ever come home and neglected your family members because you were still preoccupied with the empathic emotions you felt upon listening to a colleague's problems, you've seen the hazards of empathy overdone or done poorly.

This is the persistent argument the Yale philosophy professor Paul Bloom makes in his provocatively titled 2019 book, *Against Empathy*. Bloom writes, "For just about any human capacity, you can assess the pros and cons." And then he proceeds to highlight empathy's many cons—for example, empathy is biased; we tend to bestow it on those "who look like us, who are attractive and who are non-threatening and familiar." Bloom eagerly points out that he is not against compassion, concern, kindness, love, and morality. He's all in if that's how empathy is defined. Bloom is against empathy when it is not supported by reason and disciplined thinking, when it reflects our shortsighted and emotionally coerced responses.

I'm inclined to agree with Professor Bloom. If empathy is the capacity to "walk a mile in another person's shoes," we might reasonably ask, "Why stop after a mile? Why not two miles? Why not forever?" This is one of my bones to pick with empathy. For a personal quality bathed in such a brilliant glow of goodness, empathy certainly has a way of making us feel bad about ourselves. It asks too much of us. We feel guilty when we can't summon empathy for someone's suffering. We feel like a phony after we have parted from the object of our empathy and, no longer in their presence, have shed what we felt, as if we had been playacting at empathy, being performatively empathic but not authentically so. When do we get relief from the burden of being empathic?

But I do not want to allow such criticisms to obscure why I regard empathy as a requirement for achieving an earned life. It is not because it makes us more compassionate, moral, or kind, although those are laudable impulses.

For my purposes, empathy has few if any equals in reinforcing the paradigm we introduced in chapter 1 ("Every breath I take is a new me"), reminding us that we are an endless series of old and new versions of ourselves. Empathy's greatest utility is how effectively it reminds us to be present.

I met a speechwriter for a well-known political figure some years ago. He also published fiction and nonfiction under his own name, but when he was wordsmithing for the politician, he said he assumed the role of "professional empathist." I was impressed by the "professional" characterization. He regarded the empathy he brought to speechwriting as a discrete skill that would occupy his thoughts and emotions while he was executing the task and then easily be dropped when the job was done. He was being a total pro, doing whatever it took to do the job and then moving on. He admired the politician and agreed with him on policy and history; those were givens. He described writing in another person's voice as an "act of maximum generosity." He subsumed his personality and wrote with the client's voice and speech patterns in his ears. He said, "When I'm on the clock, every idea and every good line I have goes to the client. I don't keep a nice turn of phrase for myself to use in my own writing. It has to go into the speech." After he hands in a draft and the politician makes changes and delivers the speech, he said, "I totally forget what I wrote, as if I had been typing in a trance and then snapped out of it so I can move on to my own stuff."

The writer was describing a form of empathy most useful for achieving an earned life. While he was locked in to the client's brain and staying on task, the writer was exhibiting the empathy of understanding and feeling. Afterward, he could let go of any empathic feelings. He didn't permit them to spill over into the next episode of his ongoing life. Those feelings belonged to the old him. The new him had something new to earn. In a word, he was achieving a rare state that all of us wish we could reach more often. He was being present.

The actor and singer Telly Leung perfectly describes the mental process of compartmentalizing our empathy and being present. Telly was the star of the long-running Broadway hit *Aladdin* for two years straight. Talking about how he maintained his motivation and energy eight times a week for two years as the title character in a physically demanding production, he broke down his empathy into two parts:

First, there was his emotional empathy with the audience watching him perform. Telly said, "I was a little eight-year-old boy the first time I saw a play. I was mesmerized by the music, the singing, the dancing, and the joy. I carry the memory of that experience with me to every performance. When I go out on that Broadway stage, I think of 'little Telly' and imagine the emotions of some eight-year-old boy or girl sitting in the audience that night. I want that young person to feel what I felt. Every night, I tell myself, 'This show is for you!' "

Second is what Telly calls "authentic empathy," a respect for his colleagues when they're performing together. It's a display of professionalism that keeps him focused and "in character" for every moment of each performance. An actor trying to do his best onstage cannot afford to check out mentally or emotionally for a single second.

"In the two hours I was onstage in the role of Aladdin," Telly told me, "I had to demonstrate many extremely different emotional reactions. I had to be happy, sad, in love, rejected, serious, light-hearted, angry, and funny. I had to connect emotionally with the other actors. I had to demonstrate empathy for them every second I was onstage. Every night I had to fall in love with Princess Jasmine—and I did! When the curtain fell, I immediately shut that feeling down until the next show. Then I went home where I could resume being in love with my husband."

I cannot improve on Telly's definition. "Authentic empathy," he says, "is doing your best to be the person you need to be for the people who are with you now."

Whatever the terminology—whether the empathy is "professional" or "authentic"—the speechwriter and actor are asking the same thing of us: Are we displaying and experiencing empathy the only time it can create a positive impact, namely, when it matters in the moment?

I prefer the term *singular empathy* not only because it focuses our concern on a single person or situation, but also because it reminds us that each discrete opportunity to display our empathic powers is a unique and exceptional event. Singular empathy is unique to the moment; it changes with each situation. Sometimes it resembles the empathy of understanding, other times the empathy of feeling, caring, or doing. The only constant with singular empathy is how it concentrates our attention on a single moment and therefore makes it singular for all involved. When you demonstrate singular empathy, you cannot be inauthentic. You are not disrespecting other people from other previous moments in your life, immediate or long ago. You are demonstrating empathy to the only people who can appreciate it: the people who are with you now.

If I could have only one index card to carry with me for the rest of my life, so I could look at it any time of day as a reminder of how I should behave to achieve an earned life, this would be the message I would write on it:*

Am I being the person I want to be right now?

Do this once with an affirmative answer and you'll discover that you have earned the moment. Do this habitually and continually and you will create a string of many earned moments, stretching from days into months into years, that add up to an earned life.

---

*All credit for this idea goes to my friend and 100 Coaches member, Carol Kauffman. Thank you, Carol.

AFTER THE VICTORY LAP

———

I f you are a weekend guest at my friend Leo's house, you will eat well. Leo will ask you beforehand what you like to drink and what kind of food doesn't appeal to you, as if he were the maître d' handing out the menus and inquiring about the patrons' preferences and food allergies at a fine dining establishment.

Leo learned to cook in his early thirties when he removed himself from the labor market to stay at home taking care of his three young daughters while his wife, Robin, returned to work as a bookkeeper. After five years as a stay-at-home father, Leo joined a former colleague who was starting up a private equity firm—and remained as the firm's COO for thirty years. He worked hard, did very well, but never gave up his role as the family cook. Leo is not ostentatious about his cooking. I've never heard him describe himself as a "foodie." Only friends and family who dine at Leo's table know that cooking is his Big Reveal.

Leo's friends take his excellence at the stove for granted by now, though I doubt Leo is aware of it. If you're lucky to visit Leo and Robin for a few days at one of their many homes, you'll see how quietly industrious he is at feeding everyone. Leo is not an instinctive cook who can whip up a marvelous meal out of a hodgepodge of ingredients, like a contestant on *Iron Chef*. He scours cookbooks for recipes, knows what will work for him, and always follows a recipe to the letter—no freelance creativity allowed. Recipes that please the palate are kept in a three-ring binder that Leo consults before a meal. He plans dinners for the week, shops for all the ingredients, and prepares as much as he can in his spare time. Somehow, each meal seems better than the last. After all these years at the stove, Leo is improving.

The amazing thing about Leo is that, except when he's away from home or dining out, he does this every day—whether it's a quick meal for Robin and himself or a Thanksgiving dinner with his entire family.

Cooking is not a pursuit that Leo is realizing as a checked-off "bucket list" item that he's always wanted to do when he had the time. Leo cooked when he didn't have a job, continued when he returned to work, and didn't stop when he got really busy managing forty people and an international portfolio of investments.

Leo the cook is not a metaphor for the idea of an earned life. Leo the cook is the essence of the earned life in all its mundane magnificence.

When he wakes up in the morning, Leo is a cook. He cooks a great meal. He serves it to guests. People experience pleasure, sometimes delight. Leo feels validated seeing the bare plates and smiling faces around the table. When he wakes up the next morning, he's still a cook. He does it again.

Perhaps there is a moment after it's all over when Leo reflects with Robin about the meal. "That went well," they might agree. But that is as much of a victory lap that Leo is willing to take. He accepts that such satisfaction is fleeting. He knows he has the opportunity to earn it again with the next meal.

In this Leo is no different from any of us who have found a calling, professional or personal or avocational, that we can pursue with sufficient passion and purpose that we're eager to return to it each day. It could be the doctor trying to heal and alleviate the pain of thirty patients a day, then seeing another thirty patients the following day; or the dairy farmer rising at 4:30 A.M. to milk the herd every morning (there are no days off with a dairy herd); or the artisanal bread maker feeding the neighborhood with fresh loaves daily, or the empty-nest mother, her grown children finally living on their own, who realizes her children will always be on her mind, that she'll never cease being a mother. There is no victory lap for being a doctor, dairyman, bread maker, or mom, just the privilege and fulfillment of being those people and trying to do it to the best of their ability every day.

We should all be so lucky.

Of the various exhortations and exercises I've offered here, I'd like to highlight five recurring themes—sometimes explicitly stated but always implied—that hover over each page like guardian angels of the idea of an earned life. Each of these is readily within our control (and there are not that many things in life that we can control).

The first is *purpose.* Anything we do is more elevated, more exciting, and more connected to who we want to become if we do it with a clearly expressed purpose. (The "expressed" part makes a huge difference.)

The second is *presence.* This is the impossible ask—to be present with the people in our lives rather than missing in action. Although we can never achieve the summit of being present at all times, it's still the mountain we should never stop climbing.

The third is *community.* Accomplishing something with the help of a chosen community resonates more resoundingly, affects more people, and is often an improvement on the solo act because of the contributions of the many. Would you rather be the soloist or sing with a choir behind you?

The fourth is *impermanence*. In the grand scheme, we are here on earth for a brief moment. "We are born, we get sick, we die," said Buddha, as a reminder that nothing lasts, neither our happiness nor a day nor anything else. It is all impermanent. This is not an insight meant to depress us. It's meant to inspire us to be present and find purpose in each moment.

The fifth is *results*. This is a negative theme that reveals a positive concept—because my aim here has not been to help you become better at achieving a result. It has been to help you try your best to reach a goal. If you try your best, you have not failed, regardless of the result.

In the end, an earned life doesn't include a trophy ceremony or permit an extended victory lap. The reward of living an earned life is being engaged in the process of constantly earning such a life.

ACKNOWLEDGMENTS

I WOULD LIKE to thank the members of the 100 Coaches community who helped shape my understanding of what an earned life can be: Adrian Gostick, Aicha Evans, Alaina Love, Alan Mulally, Alex Osterwalder, Alex Pascal, Alisa Cohn, Andrew Nowak, Antonio Nieto-Rodriguez, Art Kleiner, Asha Keddy, Asheesh Advani, Atchara Juicharern, Ayse Birsel, Ben Maxwell, Ben Soemartopo, Bernie Banks, Betsy Wills, Bev Wright, Beverly Kaye, Bill Carrier, Bob Nelson, Bonita Thompson, Brian Underhill, Carol Kauffman, Caroline Santiago, CB Bowman, Charity Lumpa, Charlene Li, Chester Elton, Chintu Patel, Chirag Patel, Chris Cappy, Chris Coffey, Claire Diaz-Ortiz, Clark Callahan, Connie Dieken, Curtis Martin, Darcy Verhun, Dave Chang, David Allen, David Burkus, David Cohen, David Gallimore, David Kornberg, David Lichtenstein, David Peterson, Deanna Mulligan, Deanne Kissinger, Deborah Borg, Deepa Prahalad, Diane Ryan, Donna Orender, Donnie Dhillon, Dontá Wilson, Dorie Clark, Doug Winnie, Eddie Turner, Edy Greenblatt, Elliott Masie, Eric Schurenberg, Erica Dhawan, Erin Meyer, Eugene Frazier, Evelyn Rodstein, Fabrizio Parini, Feyzi Fatehi, Fiona MacAulay, Frances Hesselbein, Frank Wagner, Fred Lynch, Gabriela Teasdale, Gail Miller, Garry Ridge, Gifford Pinchot, Greg Jones, Harry Kraemer, Heath Dieckert, Herminia Ibarra, Himanshu Saxena, Hortense le Gentil, Howard Morgan,

Howard Prager, Hubert Joly, Jacquelyn Lane, Jan Carlson, Jasmin Thomson, Jeff Pfeffer, Jeff Slovin, Jennifer McCollum, Jennifer Paylor, Jim Citrin, Jim Downing, Jim Kim, Johannes Flecker, John Baldoni, John Dickerson, John Noseworthy, Juan Martin, Julie Carrier, Kate Clark, Kathleen Wilson-Thompson, Ken Blanchard, Kristen Koch Patel, Laine Cohen, Libba Pinchot, Linda Sharkey, Liz Smith, Liz Wiseman, Lou Carter, Lucrecia Iruela, Luke Joerger, Macarena Ybarra, Magdalena Mook, Maggie Hulce, Mahesh Thakur, Margo Georgiadis, Marguerite Mariscal, Marilyn Gist, Mark Goulston, Mark Tercek, Mark Thompson, Martin Lindstrom, Melissa Smith, Michael Canic, Michael Humphreys, Michael Bungay Stanier, Michel Kripalani, Michelle Johnston, Michelle Seitz, Mike Kaufmann, Mike Sursock, Mitali Chopra, Mojdeh Pourmahram, Molly Tschang, Morag Barrett, Naing Win Aung, Nankonde Kasonde-van den Broek, Nicole Heimann, Oleg Konovalov, Omran Matar, Pamay Bassey, Patricia Gorton, Patrick Frias, Pau Gasol, Paul Argenti, Pawel Motyl, Payal Sahni Becher, Peter Bregman, Peter Chee, Phil Quist, Philippe Grall, Pooneh Mohajer, Prakash Raman, Pranay Agrawal, Praveen Kopalle, Price Pritchett, Rafael Pastor, Raj Shah, Rita McGrath, Rita Nathwani, Rob Nail, Ruth Gotian, Safi Bahcall, Sally Helgesen, Sandy Ogg, Sanyin Siang, Sarah Hirshland, Sarah McArthur, Scott Eblin, Scott Osman, Sergey Sirotenko, Sharon Melnick, Soon Loo, Srikanth Velamakanni, Srikumar Rao, Stefanie Johnson, Steve Berglas, Steve Rodgers, Subir Chowdhury, Taavo Godtfredsen, Taeko Inoue, Tasha Eurich, Telisa Yancy, Telly Leung, Teresa Ressel, Terri Kallsen, Terry Jackson, Theresa Park, Tom Kolditz, Tony Marx, Tushar Patel, Wendy Greeson, Whitney Johnson, and Zaza Pachulia.

INDEX

Page numbers of illustrations appear in italics.

ABOUT THE AUTHOR

MARSHALL GOLDSMITH has been recognized as the world's leading executive coach and is the *New York Times* bestselling author of many books, including *What Got You Here Won't Get You There*, *Mojo*, and *Triggers*. He received his Ph.D. from the UCLA Anderson School of Management. In his coaching practice, Goldsmith has advised more than two hundred major CEOs and their management teams. He and his wife live in Nashville, Tennessee.

MarshallGoldsmith.com
Twitter: @coachgoldsmith

ABOUT THE TYPE

THIS BOOK was set in Scala, a typeface designed by
Martin Majoor in 1991. It was originally designed for a
music company in the Netherlands and then was published by the international type house FSI FontShop.
Its distinctive extended serifs add to the articulation
of the letterforms to make it a very readable typeface.

Also available from *New York Times* bestselling author

Marshall Goldsmith

"*Triggers* provides the self-awareness you need to create your own world, rather than being created by the world around you."

—ALAN MULALLY, former CEO of Ford Motor Company and one of the World's 50 Greatest Leaders (*Fortune* magazine)

Available wherever books are sold